PRAISE FOR

The Hunt: The Job of Finding Employment

"*The Hunt* is a motivating and practical guidebook for the timeless experience that we all go through finding and keeping a job. In her latest book, Jennifer Florax peels back the curtain on the intimidating and gruelling process of finding job opportunities and putting yourself forward. In the current hiring world dominated by technology and gimmicks, The Hunt focuses on building real skills that employers value and presenting your full and genuine self."

—Andrew Anderson, Anderson Business Consulting

"*The Hunt* is a straightforward and practical guide for anyone who is looking for employment, from the newly graduated to the newly on the market to those undergoing a career shift. Jennifer is a compelling storyteller and provides actionable and easy to implement advice. The Hunt will help anyone navigating the employment market for the first time or for the 10th time."

—Jennifer Cassidy

"*The Hunt* is an excellent step-by-step companion for a job seeker with its toolbox full of good advice."

—Kenneth M. Wheeler, Author of *The Other Woman: A Detective Peach Mystery*

"For someone who is starting a journey in search of a job, this is a practical and easy-to-read guide. Jennifer uses her personal experience as both the hunter and the prey to shine a light on the challenges and pitfalls of job hunting. The book contains succinct and useful tips to help improve the odds of a successful competition. A great read for the newcomers to the workforce."

—K. Siu

"A 5-star indispensable resource/blueprint for new and seasoned job seekers."

—T. Cloake, P. Eng. (retired)

"Getting into the job market at any stage in life is a daunting and stressful time in anyone's life. *The Hunt* is an easy read which is intentional and gives readers a realistic idea of what to expect and reasonable, effective and grounded strategies that work."

—Dinu Alex, Chief Disrupter, Next Evolution Ventures.

The Hunt: The Job of Finding Employment

by Jennifer Florax

ISBN 978-1-64663-691-4

Published by

köehlerbooks™

3705 Shore Drive
Virginia Beach, VA 23455
800-435-4811
www.koehlerbooks.com

the hunt

the JOB of FINDING EMPLOYMENT

JENNIFER FLORAX

VIRGINIA BEACH
CAPE CHARLES

To Dave.

Love you long time.

TABLE OF CONTENTS

Part One: Planning the Hunt

Part Two: The Hunt Doesn't Stop

AUTHOR'S NOTE

The information and lessons in *The Hunt* are a narrative of my own life experience and job-hunting efforts throughout my working career. *The Hunt* is a story about my observations of what worked with others, what didn't work, and what I simply found to be irritating behaviours by other job hunters. Sometimes I will share stories that others shared with me as I found valuable lessons within their tales. No scientific method can guarantee that any particular tips or tricks are going to land you that job you are after. What you will find in *The Hunt* is anecdotal and experience-based documentation of a lifetime of efforts. Some will work, and some may not; others are little tools to keep in your arsenal, recommended advice to help you in your *hunt*.

There is no magic bullet that will provide guarantees in your hunt. Use every bit of advice and every source of information to help with your efforts. Talk to your friends and relatives, ask for advice—heck, even ask them for a job. The point is, help is always a good thing when you are on the hunt.

PREFACE

You're surprised you are unemployed. What happened? You finished school. You got excellent grades. You had a plan, as did thousands of others. Maybe you have never had to compete for anything and competition for a job is not something you have encountered before. School is out; you are now in the real world. Things may have come easy to you in the past. Now you have to put some effort into finding a job. You probably grew up being told you can do anything in your life, through school, through childhood—which is true—but you need to take action to achieve your goals and aspirations. The process of finding a job does not follow schoolyard rules where everyone wins for merely participating in this thing called life. You are up against all your classmates who graduated when you did and are striving towards the same thing—employment.

You will feel overwhelmed; that's pretty natural. A lot of work goes into finding a job. Consider a job the *prey*, and you are the *hunter*. You stalk your prey, find out where they like to hang out, look for an opportunity, and then strike. Finding a job isn't an easy task, let alone finding one in your area of expertise. You are not only in competition with former classmates, but you are also in competition with all those who may be unemployed or underemployed, as well as those searching for a new job or a career change. Competition is stiff. Those already in the workforce have more experience than you do, which makes them more marketable.

Not to rain on your parade, but you have your work cut out for you. You need to figure out how to stand out amongst the crowd. Job hunting is the same as going to work every day. You need to put 100 percent of your effort into searching not only for employment but for the right job that fits your skill set. If you are in debt from paying for your schooling, or have a young family to support, you may not have the luxury of being particular about where you work. It may be that you have to take that crappy job to pay your bills. Once you graduate, you need to focus on building your résumé, your network of contacts, and, most importantly, your experience.

University, college, and trade schools can give you the education and basic information you need to start your career. School proves that you can be taught and have the fortitude to stick with something. It does not mean you are now the most qualified person for the job. Not to say that education is not essential, but schooling does not provide you with the skills and experience to make you qualified or successful in finding a job you want. Unfortunately, you are in the ultimate catch-22 situation; you need the experience to get a job but can't get a job because you don't have the experience. Don't get discouraged. Keep up the effort, and your time will come.

Job hunting isn't just for the young up-and-comers. There are people who go to school at all different ages these days to either reenter the workforce or change industries. Some are taking higher education for the first time at a later stage of life to improve their options for job opportunities. Some go back to school for a second or third degree, and some go right after high school. It doesn't matter how old you are—job hunting will occur at any time or stage in your life. There are many reasons and situations that people decide to enter the hunt. There are many hunters for very little prey.

There isn't a magic pill you can take. What works for one person may not work for someone else. There are things that a potential employer wants to see, but mostly, they want professionalism. It's not the big splashy thing that helps you get a job; it's the little things, like the well-written résumé, the professional mannerisms, the willingness to improve, and the desire to work. Getting a job requires effort, hard work, and a lot of setbacks before succeeding in the hunt.

HISTORY OF THE HUNT

Job hunting has changed in the last decade; consider how much the job hunt has changed over the previous 100 years, or even 500 years. With automation and innovation, many jobs are no longer needed, such as typists, lamplighters, tanners, liveries, leech collectors, or town criers, just to name a few. Some jobs still exist, like doctors, farmers, bartenders, innkeepers, professors, sailors, and soldiers. There were also, and still are, translators and book publishers.

Craftsmen such as bakers, cobblers, candlemakers, or masons once belonged to guilds. Workers were forbidden, by law, from running any business if they were not members of a guild. Only the masters were allowed to be members; apprentices in these industries were expected to earn their way into the guild to become masters, likely taking many years to accomplish that.

Sometimes one fell into a career or trade because that's what their father did. If your father was a carpenter, chances were you apprenticed under him and also became a carpenter. If your father was a farmer, you worked the farm with him until you possibly inherited the land. Choice was not a factor; you generally stayed in the particular class you were born into. This type of career path was ideal for the times, providing a way to earn a living and support a family. This situation did not promote a change in career path or rising above your station in life. To achieve something greater than the perceived status you were born into required significant determination and grit.

As time marched on, the importance of education and changing technology played significant roles in the quest for employment. These changes brought about new fields, requiring new types of workers and eliminating jobs in other industries. With the advent of electricity, manufacturing, and automation, candles became less necessary and could be made in a factory, leaving the candlemakers jobless. So how did people find jobs? You were born into it, you created it, or you worked for someone who had money to hire you. Sometimes you were snagged by the press-gang and impressed into a job without a choice in the matter. There were (and possibly still are) opportunities for daily work. One simply showed up at a place of employment to see if they were hiring for the day. Sometimes you got a job, and sometimes you didn't. And you could come back the next day and try again. Not the most permanent of situations, but some work is better than none at all.

Sometimes, to obtain employment, you either needed to be related to someone or know someone who knew someone who could vouch for you. Some people saw a sign in a window, walked into the business, and gained employment that same day, or merely showed up in the right place at the right time to gain a job. Résumés weren't a thing until the early twentieth century, and it wasn't until the 1950s that they started gaining popularity. Now, you can't get anywhere without a well-written résumé. No longer does merely wanting to work gain you the job you want. You need to possess the skills, desire, education, professionalism, and other hard or soft skills that someone else does not have simply to land the chance at a job.

Education requirements have also changed. At one point, you didn't need much more than a high school education to find a well-paying job. Few jobs have minimal education requirements and fair pay in today's job market. Postsecondary schooling is generally a minimum in most industries.

Even the way we hunt has changed. Jobs are online, requiring little human intervention in the selection process. The online hunt makes the job search much harder. A computer algorithm does not care nor understand if you are personable; this is the missing piece in today's job hunt. My advice is to use a combination of old and new methods. There is something humbling about physically walking around and asking for a job. It makes the hunt a lot more interactive and so much more satisfying if you land your prey with your fortitude and gumption.

THE CYCLE OF THE HUNT

The circumstances of the hunt change all the time. The concept of boom-and-bust has a direct relation to the availability of jobs. In boom times in the economy where jobs are plentiful, people might quit their position in the morning and have a new job by the afternoon. When demand levels are especially high, employers are so desperate for employees that they hire anyone with a modicum of skill just to ensure they have enough people to keep up with demand. The opposite of boom periods is the bust phase, when the economy has slowed down. Employers are not hiring, and jobs are less plentiful than they once were. Unfortunately, you may graduate from your postsecondary school in a period of bust, which means no matter how educated you are, there just aren't any jobs to be had. In that circumstance, your level of experience will play a more significant factor in gaining employment. Companies will not have the money to spend on providing the training you need. If you can walk in and do the job without training, you may have better success. Companies can be picky with who they hire, especially when the volume of applicants is high. A company may have one job with several hundred people applying for a single position.

Part of job hunting's cyclical nature is the change in required skill sets. What an employer needed in an employee five years ago is not the same skill set they need today. Sometimes an employer's business changes, taking a new direction and requiring different talents from their new employees than those they currently have on staff. Or the company leaves a line of business they were in, which means job losses. Demand also changes; what consumers once wanted (products and services), they may no longer desire, and if the company doesn't adjust to consumer needs, they could find themselves out of business.

Next is technology changes. Think of the changes over the last century, or the technological advances society has made even in the previous twenty years. Types of jobs that were once plentiful no longer exist. As we keep advancing, think about the number of job types currently available now, and ask yourself which of those jobs may not exist in the future. As a society, we move and change so fast, encouraging a broad level of education for new people entering the workforce, attempting to keep abreast of unforeseen changes in the market. But the reality is that while you were in school, the demand for your field may have declined, or the need isn't high anymore. As much as we like to think we can predict the future, that concept is just a pipe dream. There is no crystal ball. You can guess what the demand will be for your skill set, but there are no guarantees.

The philosophy of hiring also adapts. Through these constant cycles, it is sometimes appealing to hire graduates, those who are eager to bring their fresh ideas to a company. Then employer requirements will change again, leaning towards those with the most experience in the workforce. The economy may also impact this changing approach.

Many factors influence how successful one is in the hunt. There is no way to know for certain what influences an employer's decision. Sometimes, hunting for a job is a guessing game, sometimes it's a skill, and sometimes it's luck.

MULTIGENERATIONAL WORKFORCE

Today, learning to work in a multigenerational workforce is important. It is rare to see a company with only seasoned employees or only new graduates. Each generation has different, specific expectations of the hunt and the workplace. Sometimes a clash of expectations, work ethics, work behaviours, and experiences can appear magnified if one does not take the time to understand the impact your generation may have on your perceptions. Why is there suddenly so much focus on the differences between generations?

Expectations and attitudes towards work have changed between generations. As an example, baby boomers live to work. Work is part of their identity—how they define their role in the world. Meanwhile, millennials tend to work to live. Their expectation is to make money in order to experience other things and achieve a work-life balance. Sometimes, clashes appear in the workplace because the millennial has better things to do than working sixty hours a week, and the baby boomer may view that as not being committed to the workplace.

Baby boomers, Generation X, millennials, and Generation Z make up most of the current workforce. I won't spend time comparing and contrasting the varying needs and ideals of the different generations. Suffice to say, trying to manage the dynamic between these large age gaps is an exercise in frustration—a wasted effort. Why do we have to work or adapt to suit one generation or another? How about merely recognizing that each generation adds value and perspectives that other generations may not have? Rather than using words like *adapt* or *change*, let's consider *growth*, *learning*, or *philosophy*.

Traditionalists (they make up only a small fraction of the workforce) and baby boomers have experience and history; Generation X and millennials have new ideas and unique perspectives, and both millennials and Generation Z have the technological know-how. These groups tend to see work as a problem to be solved with technology, which can be frustrating to baby boomers and Generation X. The latter (older) groups aim to get to the root of the problem first, and they are less inclined to solve a problem technologically.

If we combine the talents of all generations, we will have one stable place to work with a wide and varied amount of experience that an employer could capitalize on. We should embrace the fact that we have such a wide range of perspectives upon which to draw. I don't mean give everyone everything they want, nor do I suggest we stick with what we know and change nothing. We should strive for balance, respecting the past, the knowledge, the history, and the experiences of the older generations, while aiming to acknowledge the newer generations' diversity and varied opinions—adding value to the workplace as a whole.

There is also a group of people who are hard to quantify—people who chronologically fit into one group of workers but don't match that group's attributes. These people seem to straddle one or more of the generations in terms of their values and characteristics. They may have the work habits of a baby boomer but the technological savvy of a millennial. This group may or may not struggle with the chronological classification, and depending on who it is, they may relate better to a different type of worker.

No matter the generation, we should embrace the opportunity that their knowledge, experience, and perspective offers.

MY HUNT

My hunt has been a long and arduous journey. I had the same difficulties most have when trying to find a job. As my life changed, I needed different positions for different reasons and changed jobs because life circumstances changed. I have learned many lessons throughout my job hunt; some I learned quicker than others. But every lesson can be applied to every job I have searched for.

I've been working since I was fourteen. It wasn't always easy to get a job, no matter how old I was. To be honest, without my mom, I probably wouldn't have had my first job. She got it for me through her network of people and with the simple question "Are you hiring?" Lesson number one—accept any help offered. At fourteen, the thought of a dream job didn't enter my mind, and it still hasn't. I'm still waiting to figure out what I want to be when I grow up. There are even times I find it hard to believe I am an adult. But enough digressing. My first job was as a dishwasher in a bakery. My mom knew the owner and asked them to hire me, resulting in a summer job with pretty good hours. That's when I figured out making money was cool. When the job ended, and I went back to school for the fall, I realized I missed making money, and that's when my real hunt started.

I got the next job on my own. Growing up in a small town, there were only so many things a teenager was qualified to do. So, my next job was at a clothing store. It was definitely not my dream job, but it served its purpose in providing spending money. I was there two years, which is pretty dependable for a teenager, but again, there weren't many places to go. After the clothing store, my next job was at the convenience store. And I can say *the* convenience store because there was only one. It was a fun job—lots to do, people coming and going, lots of hours, and fair pay for the time.

But then the end of high school came. I had to enter the real world, and it was a little scary. I moved to a larger city, and the need for a job took on a whole new meaning. I no longer needed a position to have spending money; I needed a job to survive. The safety net of my parents was gone. It was the early 1990s. Remember how we talked about the economy? The economy was in a downturn; jobs were hard to find. I've lost track of the number of jobs I had, which didn't last—for many reasons. Sometimes the business was sold, sometimes it was a lousy job, sometimes the business went bankrupt, and sometimes there just wasn't enough work for all the employees. I worked in several fast-food places and video stores. I was a telemarketer, and I even tried door-to-door sales. The number of different interviews I had amazes even me.

Lesson number two—if it sounds too good to be true, it probably is. When you are looking for a job, you sometimes feel so desperate that you will jump at anything that seems like it will make you lots of money for minimal effort. Lesson number three—if a company asks you to pay money for the privilege of working for them, it's not a real job. This is how those companies make money, scamming people desperate for work.

After a series of service-type jobs, I figured it was time for me to find a better fit, something a bit more stable than the service industry. It wasn't easy to do at the time. So how did I do this? I wrote a résumé and printed about 100 copies. Then I hit the pavement. And by hitting the pavement, I mean I looked for a cluster of businesses that I was interested in and walked to each one to ask if they were hiring. Looking in person is much different than cold-calling, which is probably the most challenging way to job hunt. The company may not actively be looking for a new employee—but you could get lucky. If this is your only option, it's always best to try.

I also looked in the newspaper for job advertisements. I don't believe I had a car at the time. I hopped on public transport, traveled an hour or so just to apply in person, and hoped to make an impression. It eventually paid off, and I got a job that provided a learning opportunity. That job finally gave me some of the stability I was looking to gain. It was suitable for a substantial period of time, but then life happened. And by life, I mean buying a house and having a baby. These life changes once again adjusted my criteria in my job hunt. I wanted more advancement opportunities and the prospect of more income. With a family, you want more than stability; you hope for security and a fair wage.

So, I started the hunt again. This time, I was looking for something entry-level, with room to grow and advance, with additional opportunities to make a higher wage (more stability). But getting a job at a company that allows room to grow doesn't mean your job hunt ends. Jobs are not handed out because you want them or because you've been there the longest. You still have to put in the effort, write a résumé, apply, interview, and go through the entire process. Even within a single company, the number of applications I've submitted is significant. Just because you're there and have the experience does not mean the job is yours for the taking. It's still a hunt. You still need to be relevant and competitive, bringing your A game every time.

At one point, while unemployed and job hunting, I became desperate. I wanted a change or an opportunity to grow, advance, or learn more. And still, more often than not, an opportunity came up that was just too good to pass up. While looking for a job, I didn't give much thought to landing a dream job, nor was that part of my criteria as I hunted. Not a lot of people have the luxury of working as a hobby; most are working to provide for themselves and their family, which means that you will do whatever it takes for security. If you happen to find that job that is your dream and meets your other criteria, then hang on to it; you're one of the lucky ones.

I share my story because I'm sure it's relatable to many. Job hunting isn't the easiest task. The reason a person needs or wants a job changes throughout their life; recognizing those needs will help with the hunt in the long term—enhancing your focus and assisting in targeting your desired job.

Part One

PLANNING THE HUNT

Planning your hunt is like any other preparation for an adventure. Get yourself in the right frame of mind. Think about your goal, what you want to get out of it, and where you see yourself working. Identify your prey. What are you going after, what do you want, and why you want it? What is the purpose or intention that you are looking to achieve? Identify a clear hunting ground. Select the industry, type of business, and geographical location. Prepare your tools—mainly your résumé and your attitude. Adjust your mindset and use every resource in your tool chest while on your HUNT.

THE RÉSUMÉ

Your résumé is the most crucial document you need to create. In many instances, your résumé is the potential employer's first impression of you. In other cases, it may be their only impression of you. Your résumé should reflect you and your skills, demonstrating why you are the person this company should be hiring. You are one of many people applying for the job; you have no idea how many people you are up against or what their skill sets might be. You need to use your résumé to stand out.

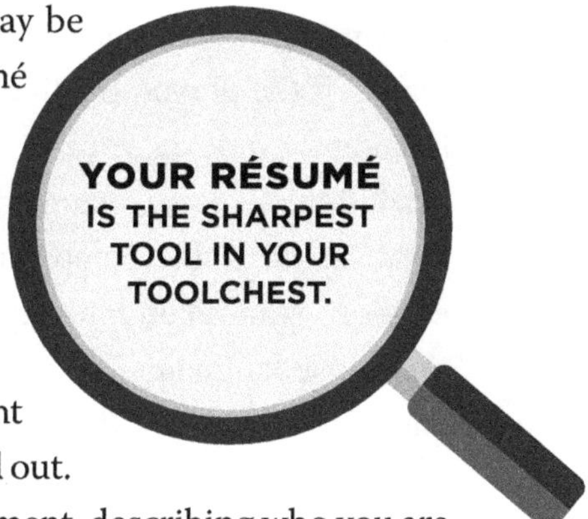

Consider your résumé as your advertisement, describing who you are, what you can do, and why you fit within the organization. Use it to sell yourself.

Your résumé should not be a canned version that you send to every potential employer. Every version of your résumé should be tailored to meet the qualifications listed in the job advertisement. Highlight your skills; the potential employer should not have to search for your skills buried within the résumé. Simply throwing words on a page and hoping some of them stick doesn't help sell yourself as the best candidate for a job. It bears repeating: your résumé is a representation of you. Make a good impression.

CLEAR AND CONCISE

Ensure your résumé only includes relevant information. Erase the unnecessary details. Résumé writing is a lot of work and very time-consuming. It is very tempting to write a generic version, to provide blanket information that could be sent out to several companies, but it should be specific to the industry. Once you've narrowed down the scope of your search, the foundational information on your résumé won't change that much.

It is tempting to fill up your résumé, using as many words as you know, hoping to make it look impressive. However, it is more important to ensure the person reading your résumé can understand what skills you would bring to their organization. Providing convoluted information about yourself is just an exercise in frustration for the reader. If the person reading your résumé can't find the skills they're looking for quickly, your résumé will end up on the NO pile without hesitation. A messy résumé does not exude confidence that you know what you are doing. Keep in mind, your competitors' résumés may be easier to read. Plain language is your friend. Using jargon or forcing grandiose language can appear haphazard or like you're trying too hard. Be meticulous with the words you choose. Write in simple terms, with small words, easy flow, and short action words; this will keep the reader of your résumé engaged.

JUST THE FACTS

Whatever you choose to include in your résumé must be true; any skills you list must be supported by evidence. If asked, you can provide an example of what you did, how you did it, and why it was important. If you cannot substantiate the skills you have listed, it could be considered a fabrication; then it begs the question—what else in your résumé is not valid? Stick to the facts and only include relevant attributes. Nobody wants to know what your hobbies are. The hiring manager does not need to know that you like to paint or take long walks on the beach. If it's not relevant to the job, don't take up space on your résumé.

KEEP IT SIMPLE & CLEAR. WHO DID YOU WORK FOR AND WHAT DID YOU DO THERE?

Some people say that all résumés must start with an objective; I disagree. Remove the objective from your résumé, as it's obvious the objective is to get the job. If I were reading your résumé, I wouldn't want to read any profound statements or declarations of your aspirations. It boils down to you wanting a job. I can't imagine an employer who would get excited over really long résumés, filled with extra, irrelevant information. Take a moment to think about what the employer has to read. They have one job available and have received a couple hundred applicants. Do they want to read a few concisely written résumés or several that are each the length of a novel? Receiving a six-page résumé with a page and a half of extra details can be very irritating. Keep it factual, to the point, and relevant to the job.

Again, make sure your facts are correct. If you state you have a diploma or a degree, you better be able to prove it. If somebody hired you into a position based on information from your résumé, and that statement proves to be inaccurate, you'll suffer the consequences (most likely, you'll be fired). Most places of employment do not want disingenuous people working for them. If you can't be trusted with something as simple as your résumé, how can you be trusted to have the company's best interests in mind?

FORMAT

As mentioned earlier, you need to make your résumé stand out from the hundreds of others. Standing out does not mean you need fancy designs, flowers, or other strange patterns. And don't spritz your résumé with perfume. As you format your résumé, check for things like text orientation, consistent font, and the alignment of bulleted content. Information within your bulleted lists should start with an action word, such as *ability*, *experience*, or *knowledge*, and should be in an active voice. Do not be vague with statements such as "may be able to" or "some experience." Cross-reference the content of your text with your format. If you include excellent attention to detail as a skill but have used several different fonts throughout your document, you don't have excellent attention to detail. Also, check your spelling. In this day and age of spell-check, there is no reason for spelling errors.

Put all your jobs in descending and chronological order. Your first job, especially if you have been in the job market a while, may not be relevant to the current job you are applying for. The potential employer wants to see where you are working right now. Next, they want to see a succession of your previous jobs, which support the declaration that you have the skills and experience for the job. An unorganized résumé with past jobs in no particular order speaks to a disorganized mind. Again, if a hiring manager has to dig through vast volumes of information to look for your experience and skills, it will not be worth their time. They will probably end up choosing a competitor for the position.

Make sure you have detailed your responsibilities in each of your previous jobs. Just providing a list of employment does not provide any information on successive learning. Did you learn more at each job? Or have you had progressively more experience at each position? These elements are important to include in your well-formatted résumé.

It can be difficult to read a résumé with skills listed in one place and jobs listed in another. Make it easy for the reader to understand what jobs were performed and what skills you used at that position. If the potential employer contacts one of your prior companies, listing skills in the same location as that job will allow them to ask appropriate questions regarding your responsibilities with that company. Any extra skills you have can be captured in the cover letter.

EDUCATION

One of the very first screening criteria for any job is your education. Make sure you list all relevant education you may have. If you are a seasoned employee and have already had a full career, no one wants to know if you graduated high school. If you are newly graduated, then that is relevant education to include. If you are currently in school, at a university, college, or trade school, state that in your résumé. Include any relevant courses that pertain to the job. Being in school does not always preclude you from applying for a job. Going to school and working at the same time demonstrates determination. Completely changing careers is another reason to add your schooling. This makes you attractive to a potential employer; you may offer a wealth of knowledge they could tap into.

Again, don't include irrelevant schooling. No one needs to know you are taking Spanish lessons unless this job requires speaking Spanish. Don't include your interests, like photography or skydiving lessons, unless those skills are relevant to the potential workload. While intriguing, it may not further your quest for employment.

If you have taken some one-off courses, don't list every single one. In the current environment of continuous learning, this could turn into an entire page of your résumé. Keep only the ones you think a future employer might be interested in. This would be relevant if you are a mechanic by trade and took a small engine repair course or if you are a secretary and took speed-reading or minute taking. But if you were a secretary who took small engine repair (and you weren't a secretary at a mechanic shop), it's best to exclude it from the list.

As technology changes, employers expect potential employees to "just know" how to use programs like Word or Pages and spreadsheets. While you don't need to include the courses on the list (it's expected that most people know how to use those without formal education), it can still be a good idea to take the course—guarantee you know how to use the programs. This is important if you're asked in the interview; you'll be able to speak to this education.

THE COVER LETTER

Once you start to move into the professional realm, a cover letter is essential. Cover letters demonstrate the effort that you have put into the job hunt. Merely having a résumé that you recycle for every job is no longer enough in a professional environment. You can have a basic set of résumé information that you simply keep up to date, but you should use the cover letter to shine.

The cover letter can describe why you are the best fit for a job, especially if you do not have all the skills listed in the job advertisement. This is where you can describe what you have done similarly in other jobs, adding more details. You can also speak to other experiences that the company may find valuable, hitting all the job description points. The cover letter also shows your personality and provides you an opportunity to build rapport with the employer. The body of the résumé can be used to understand the skill sets of the applicant, and the cover letter can be used to see what else this person can do.

The cover letter is also an excellent indicator of the writing capabilities of the applicant. It can demonstrate if the applicant can format a letter correctly, use the proper forms of address, or write eloquently, allowing the employer to gauge articulation skills in a written document. Think of the cover letter as another test of your skills. Did you understand what the job is about? Can you describe what you can do in a written format, can you get your message across, and are you able to provide supporting statements?

The cover letter is probably a better place to speak to your interest in working for a particular company than an objective statement. Using the cover letter as a forum, you can articulate your aspirations for this job, why you are the right candidate, and why you want to work for this company. The trick with this is balance. You want to be genuine, but don't oversell, as you can come off as either desperate or cocky. Let's face it; everyone thinks they are the "best person for the job."

GAPS IN YOUR RÉSUMÉ

Potential employers look at the gaps in your résumé. People will compare your education to your work experience to see what you were doing during the gap years. If you have a couple of years where it appears you were not working, you will need to explain. If you say something along the lines of "I took a year to find myself," you have just labelled yourself as flighty and unreliable. Better explanations are "I was on maternity leave" or "I was in school" or some other reason that makes you sound responsible. If you have taken time off to build homes in another country, don't leave that off your résumé. Include it as part of your experience. It makes you more human and responsible. The point is, ensure that there is a full account of your time in the workforce.

JOB HOPPING

Some people believe they need to continuously mix it up and look for a new job every couple of years. Many years ago, an acquaintance once told me that her mother had advised her to never stay in a job longer than a year. In my opinion, that was very poor advice. Employers who see a résumé with many different positions and very short work terms may question the applicant's ability to stick with a job. I personally wouldn't want to hire someone that I know is going to leave. The hiring process is long, complicated, and expensive. It is not a process that companies like to undertake. Once a company has someone in place, they put time, money, and effort into training. Training a new person is a significant investment, and employers want to see some return on that investment, meaning the employee will stick around and perform the duties required. They want to hire someone reliable and whom they can depend on to ensure the work gets done. In reality, it takes at least a year to have a complete understanding of your job. Then it takes another couple of years to get to the point where your job becomes second nature and does not require much thought. Once you have arrived at the point where you are so comfortable that you can do your job in your sleep, enjoy that for a bit, rather than rushing off to something new. Every six years or so is a good span between jobs.

Someone with a new job every year or two, and in extreme cases, every six months, presents as disloyal to the company for which they work; consider this a red flag for a future employer. It may be that you think this is expanding your experience, but it isn't. You aren't there long enough to learn anything or implement the few things you have learned.

If you are genuinely doing short-term work, this will need an explanation. You could state that the job listed was a project and note the duration. Or include that it was a temporary job, and make sure to explain why. Or, if you are a contract worker, list the leading company and the positions under that leading company. Listing successive six-month positions without explanation does not allow the potential employer to understand the whole story of your work history.

Be as concise and succinct as you can, while sharing enough to tell your job story. Your résumé is the linear story of you and your work history and is the opportunity to shine a light on your skills. Be sure to tell the whole story of you, including your experience and what you will bring to the job.

BEGINNING THE HUNT

Job hunting requires more than sitting in front of a computer. Sure, there are many job sites out there that will email you a notification when jobs matching your pre-set qualifications become available. And yes, many companies prefer that you apply online. Applying online, though, makes you one of the many bits of data within the system. It does not allow you to stand out among the crowd.

Using all methods of job hunting, both tried-and-true and new, will do nothing but expand your opportunities to find a job. In person is always your best option if available. Personal interaction with potential employers allows you to provide information that is not apparent through a résumé or an online application.

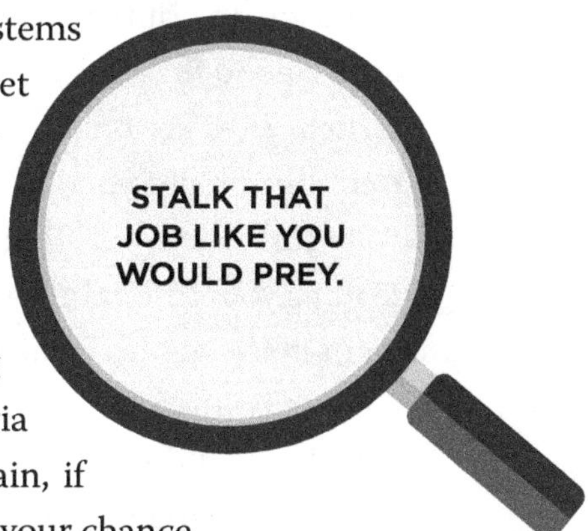

Many of the online application systems will screen your résumé based on a set criterion. If you don't match precisely with what the computer program is looking for, it could very well knock you out of the running for a job—qualified or not. There could also be pre-screening questions, which may be the only criteria to move your application forward. Again, if you don't match precisely, you have lost your chance.

Direct and personal interactions allow the potential employer to understand who you are as a person and as a possible future employee. Personal interaction will set you apart from online computer personas. Employers create a perception of their potential candidates via the online personality they see. You need to use that opportunity to get your foot in the door and then set yourself apart on a more personal level.

Not to discourage you, but hunting for a job is disheartening, endless, frustrating, and a lot of work. The volume of effort required to even search for a job can be pretty taxing, let alone customizing your résumé for each application or preparing for an interview. However, it is a very satisfying feeling when you land that job—a significant achievement and a great accomplishment.

ONLINE

Online can mean any number of search engines, company websites, job boards, online forums, or any other electronic means of searching for a job. This is an excellent place to start, as these sites will give you an idea of the job availability within your field and may also provide options or opportunities you weren't aware of before. Company websites are probably the most reliable place to start if you know where you want to work. Generally speaking, they post available positions with very detailed job descriptions, giving you a good indication of whether you may be a good fit.

These sites are only a start to your search, not the only place to search. Essentially, you have parked yourself in front of a computer and are surfing the net. There is not a lot of physical effort required in uploading your résumé and clicking a few buttons. You have absolutely no skin in the game. Think of online job hunting as your map, your beginning point, or your plan to start the process of hunting for a job. Remember that this is the same place that everyone else looking for a job is starting. You need to take extra steps to stand out.

Many companies only accept online applications. They do not want to see people until they are ready. They are not interested in taking numerous paper copies of résumés and applications. Additional effort is required to make sure that your online presence outshines all other applicants, and this does not mean you should use a cat emoji as your online avatar, nor should you write your résumé in a strange, purple font. Using specific wording and language that is geared towards the job will focus the potential employer on your application instead of someone else's. Use this opportunity to market your skill sets and to demonstrate your desire to work at this company. Sometimes it's possible to provide more than your résumé, such as an introduction via the application process. If there is a question within the application that asks why you want the job, make sure you answer it—don't skip the question. Have a well-thought-out answer that reflects the company's values and provides the reader with a sense that you've done your homework and can demonstrate that you know the company well. Don't say something like "Because I need a job" or "I hate my current job." That's just going to get you in the NO pile. Be sensible but memorable. Be intuitive but thoughtful; do just enough to stand out but not enough that you are deemed eccentric.

BE ANNOYING

Be annoying but not over-the-top annoying. Annoying, in this instance, means making it known that you want to work for this company. Being annoying is not usually well received in a professional environment because no one will want to talk to you if you are genuinely irritating. However, for service industry jobs, this may be a good thing. Turnover within the service industry is generally high. On top of the turnover rate, some employers also receive hundreds of applications in a month—whether they are looking for employees or not. Weeding through the volume of applications is a monumental task.

If you check back on your applications or apply to the same job several times, you may become annoying. Still, you have also demonstrated your eagerness to work. Even if there aren't any positions available at the moment, you have created a situation where the manager remembers who you are. When jobs become available, you may be at the top of the pile to call for an interview, so personal interaction is essential. If you check on your application several times and ask to speak with the manager each time, you will develop a personal relationship. The manager will get to know who you are personally and be more apt to interview you when a position becomes available.

Don't become a pest. Checking every day is too much, but checking every couple of weeks may be sufficient (depending on the industry). If you are relatively sure there is a high turnover or they hire in large batches of people, you may need to check more often for openings. If this business has a job board (a job board is a physical location that lists or provides descriptions of the available jobs), you need to view it in person; you could, theoretically, check every week.

In any case, you have made it known that you are interested in working and have demonstrated that you are willing to put in effort. I once visited a company every couple of weeks, met some really nice people, and started to look forward to our visits. I never did get the job, but I was able to refer other people to the company who did find employment there.

COLD CALLING

Cold-calling is one of the most challenging ways of job hunting. This activity involves approaching companies that have not advertised that they are looking to hire. Cold-calling is hard to do because you don't necessarily have an in with the company. There may not be a reason for you to be there other than to ask for employment. Sometimes you will be stuck leaving your résumé at the front door. Sometimes

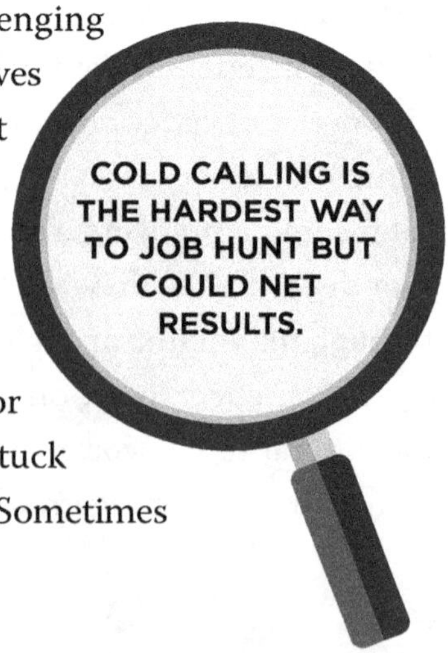

the company will blow you off altogether with no opportunity to talk to anyone, much less the opportunity to leave your résumé. At times, someone might have a brief conversation with you; maybe they take your résumé, or maybe they show you to the door. Take any opportunity to talk to whomever you can, regardless of their current hiring stance. This includes people who are not in charge of hiring; you never know if they have some influence.

At one of my jobs, people dropped off résumés all the time. In a very small office, each of us could have been on the receiving end of the résumé. We were required to speak with each person and put a small *yes* or *no* on every résumé so the boss had our first impression. Every opportunity is a chance to leave an impression. To be specific, you want to leave a good impression. You do not want to come off as overly pushy or aggressive. You want the manager to remember you fondly when they decide to hire next.

You may find yourself pounding the pavement, especially if you are not particular about where you want to work. You could have a stack of résumés that you hand out to businesses you're remotely qualified to work for. This is not the most comfortable or successful way of job hunting, but what is the worst that could happen? You had a nice walk, met some lovely people, and successfully handed out a few résumés. You could get a job for that effort.

TEMPORARY WORK

Temporary jobs are a perfect way to make an impression, demonstrate your skills, get paid, and gain experience all at the same time. The company you are working for may not hire you full time right now but will think of you for future opportunities. You need to give 100 percent of your effort if hired for a temporary job. Viewing the job as temporary and not putting in the same effort you would in a non-temporary position does not enhance your reputation as a good worker. Many people may hesitate to take temporary work, primarily because their job hunt still isn't over. The temporary job gives you some breathing room, but most people want the security of knowing where their paychecks will be coming from on a more permanent basis. Always treat a temporary job as your own, as though you were never going to leave the position. Some temporary assignments have the genuine potential to turn into a permanent job. You are not usually privy to why the work is temporary to begin with; if you treat this job as if it isn't going to end, it might not.

If you have many short-term assignments, be clear on your résumé that these jobs were temporary or project work. Otherwise, it appears that you are unreliable and can't stick with a job, gaining the title of job-hopper. There are so many benefits to temporary work. Just ensure that you are clear with potential employers what these positions are, what you did there, and why you aren't there any longer.

NETWORKING

Networking is usually easier to do when you have an established network of contacts. Networks typically develop over time through the people you meet during your different employment positions. Keeping professional and casual relationships will help you in future job searches. Not only will your contacts keep you abreast of any potential job openings, but they may also recommend you for an opportunity. Again, doing a good job can open future doors no matter where you are. If these contacts know your work, skills, ethics, and other attributes, you will have a leg up on the competition. As mentioned, a temporary position will assist in developing and expanding your network of contacts. Use any opportunity to create a good work reputation. This effort will only benefit you in the future.

Networking means putting yourself out there and making an effort to talk to people. If you are incredibly introverted, this is hard to do. Overcoming shyness and a reserved personality will make this exercise difficult but not impossible. You can do it; it just takes practice. Start with your current close circle and have them introduce you to others, maybe in smaller settings. Your network will organically grow in your existing work environment as you have more interactions with people through daily work. You could have an extensive network in a large organization without really going outside of your comfort zone. Although difficult as a more reserved person, this might benefit you in the long run as this organic approach does not overwhelm you.

Take some examples from your neighbouring extrovert colleagues. Often times, it is about finding a balance. For instance, extroverts may have an easier time with networking, but there is such a thing as too much. Extroverts can be over the top and come off as aggressive or disingenuous. If you are an extrovert, tone it down sometimes.

Some people simply have a knack for networking. They are genuine, know how to put people at ease, know all the right things to say, and enjoy meeting new people. They make the task of networking look easy. These are the schmoozers who can gain attention as soon as they enter the room—not sleezy people, but people who automatically click with others. I know I envy those people and their ease in any situation.

HEADHUNTERS

Headhunters are one way to go. However, most headhunting companies search for those already in the workforce at mid-level or executive management positions. Employers will contact a headhunting company when they have specific requirements for a particular job that may be hard to fill or has a high salary level. If you are at this level or looking to move up, it's a good idea to speak to a headhunter, especially if you are planning on leaving your current position. Speaking to a headhunter will open some doors on your behalf or at least give you a sense of the available jobs. First-time job seekers most likely will not fit into this category; however, this is an option once you are more established in your career path.

JOB AGENCIES

Job agencies or staffing agencies are businesses that supply temporary or contract workers to other companies. Generally, this is temporary work to help with a project, to cover the work of an absent employee, or when an abundance of work needs to get done within a short period of time. Although these agencies specialize in short-term work assignments, they sometimes help with résumé writing, interview skills, or other necessary training, such as typing skills. Even though these assignments are short, they are good opportunities to build a network of contacts for the future. Doing an excellent job as this temporary assignment could lead to a more permanent position.

Don't limit yourself to one agency. Apply at a few to broaden your chances. As an employment agency is also a business, expect to be interviewed by them as well. They generally play the intermediary between you and other companies. You will usually not have an interview with the company you are placed with unless it's for a permanent position.

ATTITUDE

Your attitude towards hunting for a job will be a significant factor in whether or not you find one. Sitting back and hoping for a job that pays $2,000 a day isn't reasonable. There are no quick ways or guarantees to ensure you get a job offer. Any technique you use to hunt for a job or land one (or, for that matter, even stay in a position) requires effort on your part. Your attitude towards the process of hunting for employment will be the deciding factor for your success.

If you are serious about the hunt, you need to treat a job hunt just like a regular job.

Have a plan of action to help determine where to focus your efforts, what industry you are targeting, and, sometimes, even what company you want to work for. You can even go so far as to schedule what you are doing each day to help yourself get a job. These activities do not include sleeping until noon and then checking your email, hoping that the job offer came through. It means getting up early to pound the pavement (or the keyboard). You have to use a variety of methods.

Keeping a positive frame of mind will also help in the hunt for a job. If you start to become jaded or pessimistic about the effort required (and you will), that attitude will come through in every interaction you have with potential employers. Continually remind yourself that the job hunt takes time and a lot of it; these things don't happen overnight. And once you finally find an opportunity, hiring managers usually do not make snap decisions to hire someone. Patience is required at all stages in the process.

FIRST IMPRESSIONS

The sad reality of the job hunt, including the interview process, is that the person calling the shots has potentially made up their mind about you within the first thirty seconds of meeting you. First impressions are made in several ways. If you have submitted your résumé directly to this person, you have a chance to introduce yourself to the potential employer personally and maybe strike up a conversation. You may have a mini interview on the spot. If you make a favourable impression, you may have another opportunity to further this relationship at a future interview. The good impression you make will stick in a potential employer's mind as they short-list their stack of résumés for interviews.

When applying for a job, you don't always submit your application or résumé to the person in charge of hiring. Sometimes you only speak with a front-facing person who has no influence on the hiring for a position. However, this does not mean you can be rude to the receptionist. Whoever you speak to will be the one handing your résumé over, and they will take note of your attitude.

Following up on the application may net you an opportunity to have a short meeting with your future employer. This is another open opportunity to demonstrate your commitment to wanting to work and display your interest in working for the company. You have a chance to make an impression before the other candidates have even thought to do so. Most don't consider following up on the status of their application. Again, don't make too much of a pest out of yourself. Checking once or twice is alright, but don't phone or stop by every day.

In many instances, the one and only time you meet the hiring manager is during the interview. How you answer questions is just as important as what information you provide. Be confident but not cocky. Be informed but not a know-it-all. Be concise but completely answer the questions. There is no do-over for first impressions, so make the one opportunity you get a good one.

HOW TO DRESS

As much as we would like to deny it, many first impressions are made based on how we look—not in terms of race, gender, culture, or any other typical stereotypes that first come to mind, but in terms of your attire. No matter the type of job you are interviewing for, you should always strive to look professional. Even if you are interviewing for a retail position as a stock handler with no interaction with the public, you need to make an impression. If you show up in jeans and a T-shirt, you may leave an unfavourable image. At the very least, always wear dress pants and a nice shirt. The further up the corporate ladder you are applying, the more professional you should look. For ladies and men alike, a business suit is the way to go. A woman might have more to choose from in the clothing department, but for men, you can't go wrong with a suit and tie. You shouldn't wear leggings, golf shirts, see-through tops, khakis, or miniskirts. And if your first thought is *I gotta be me,* then you don't want the job that badly. A job interview is not the place to

> **LOOK THE PART OF A PROFESSIONAL. DRESS APPROPRIATELY, WHEN YOU JOB HUNT AND WHEN YOU INTERVIEW.**

express yourself. When applying for a job in person, you need to look the part, like someone genuinely ready to work—not like someone who just rolled out of bed and is casually looking for a job.

BE GENUINE

In all instances and interactions, be genuine. People in general, regardless of whether or not they are employers, can tell when you are faking it. Don't put on a performance you can't live up to. Don't oversell your skills with no hope of ever delivering. Don't sell yourself short either; talk up what you know you can excel at. If you are hired, who you are in the interview needs to be the person who shows up on the first day of work. Too often, people who are not genuine during the hiring process become a pain to work with by week one. Do not merely regurgitate a job advertisement because you think that's what the hiring manager wants to hear. Be informed of what you can do and how it applies to the job the company seeks to fill. Don't think that flattering the potential employer will ensure success in the process. You need to live up to the promises you made in the interview.

Being genuine means being honest and sincere in your interactions with people, essentially treating others the way you want to be treated. Be genuine in your questions; ask to learn, not to flatter. A genuine desire to work and do a good job will get you much farther than empty platitudes.

THE HANDSHAKE

The handshake seems like a trivial item to focus on, but more is conveyed in a handshake than you imagine. A handshake can be the moment a potential boss decides whether they like you or not. Your whole career could be built on what kind of impression you leave. Thirty seconds (and a two-second handshake) could make or break you.

The first handshake can set the tone for the rest of the relationship between interviewer and interviewee. A loose or limp handshake can engender a perception that you lack confidence in your abilities. A handshake where your hand is more on top of the person whose hand you are shaking may show dominance. Shaking hands as though you don't want to touch anyone can suggest that either you think you are better than others or you simply don't like people in general. Shaking a woman's hand as though you are in an eighteenth-century parlour is not flattering to the woman. It can appear condescending. Also, you don't want to hang on to the other person's hand too long—that's just weird and uncomfortable for everyone.

A handshake should be no longer than a couple of seconds. It should be firm and demonstrate confidence but not so hard that you hurt the person. It should convey the thankfulness to be included in the interview process and a genuine interest in meeting the prospective employer.

GHOSTING

I had no idea ghosting was a real thing. I've read a few articles on it, but I honestly thought it was one of those urban legends. Ghosting on a date, I understand, though it's tacky; it just never occurred to me as something that actually happens in a professional environment. You don't know it's real until it happens to you. Ghosting is when a prospective candidate is simply a no-show, or when a new hire simply doesn't show up for their first day of work. I've even read that people leave for lunch and never come back.

To be honest, I am not sure why anyone would go through the trouble of writing a résumé, booking the interview, and pre-screening, and then just not show up. They wasted not only the prospective employer's time but also their own. Ghosting does not leave a favourable impression. Employers will start keeping records of those who are no-shows for either work or interviews. Continue this behaviour, and the available job opportunities are going to shrink. Not only will jobs disappear, but people won't even review your résumé because you have a reputation of not showing up. Leaving the impression that you are not dependable will further reduce your chances of landing a job in a bust economy.

I'm not sure why anyone would want to squander any potential for a job, whether you already got an offer or not. Even if you did receive a different or better offer, at least have the courtesy to phone and decline. This gives the potential employer a better impression and allows them the ability to find another candidate. Being up front about your change in circumstances also leaves the door open for future job opportunities. In this instance, honesty is the best policy. Suggest that the relationship be kept open for any future opportunities. Instead of ghosting, use the opportunity to network.

REFERENCE CHECKS

The reference check is another assessment to determine if you fit with the company. References are an essential tool for the potential employer, to gauge the technical skills, the potential, and the personality of the candidate. Reference checks include tactical-type questions: Did Sally show up to work on time? Was Sally ever missing in action? What kind of effort did Sally put into her daily duties?

When checking references, your new potential employer might also ask your former supervisors how you handled the pressure, your customers or clients, and what you do when faced with a challenge. How did you interact with your coworkers, or why did you leave that job? These are all indicators of whether or not the supervisor will want to hire you. If you put a name as a reference, make sure they give you a good one. Just because you worked with or for someone doesn't mean they're going to give you a good reference. If you left on bad terms, don't expect a glowing recommendation.

You should also always ask your reference before listing them as one. Put yourself in the employer's shoes; it will make you look unprepared if you don't warn your reference, if your reference doesn't remember you, or if they seem surprised by the call. These potential references won't be prepared and may not give the impression you are looking for. It's also essential that your reference will be available to talk. Spending a week or more trying to get ahold of a reference may disqualify you from the running. If the employer can't verify your skills, you may not be considered.

The person you ask to be your reference should genuinely want to be your reference. If your reference has no interest in speaking with anyone, this will not help your case in the job hunt.

DON'T USE YOUR MOM OR YOUR FRIEND

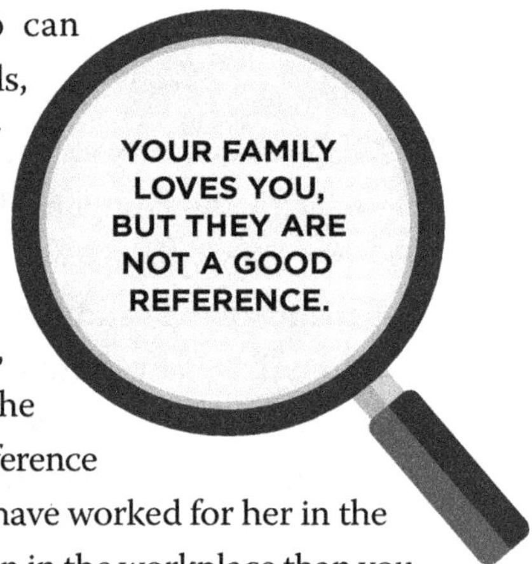

The best reference is someone who can provide an accurate overview of your skills, behaviours, attitude, and aptitude for learning, such as a previous employer or someone who has supervised your work in the past. Your mom is not a reference. She may love you and want you to succeed, but she's not a judge of your effort in the work environment, and having her as a reference doesn't appear professional (even if you have worked for her in the past). Generally, you are a different person in the workplace than you are with your family. Your mom has no real idea about what you can do in a job situation.

The same goes for your friends. Sometimes you will use a colleague as a reference, which is okay in normal circumstances, but if they are your friend too, the objectivity is taken away, and they may not be as unbiased as the prospective employer would want them to be. If a coworker is your reference, make sure it was someone you worked closely with. They can speak to your skill set and the work that you completed. Hopefully, this person can be objective enough to provide the appropriate kind of reference.

You also do not want to use a friend who would throw you under the bus to get ahead. Make sure you know who you are providing as a reference.

CURRENT AND PAST SUPERVISORS

The best indicator of your work habits is someone who has supervised your work. These people will have a better frame of reference. Anyone who has managed your work will speak to your work's performance, attitude, and quality. If the name you provide cannot offer this information, it could be considered an invalid reference.

If you have never had a job, it can be challenging to find an appropriate reference. However, teachers, professors, or anyone who has provided you guidance in some fashion, and who is not a relative, would be the right choice. If you volunteered for an organization and had to report to someone, this would also be a suitable choice as a reference. An alternative option is anyone who has provided you direction, supervised your output, or can speak to your work ethic and behaviour. I mentioned to my kids that they could use a neighbour as a reference, particularly if they have helped that neighbour with things like yard work. It's still an example of work. There are always other choices out there; you just have to look for them.

NAME-DROPPING

Picking someone with a powerful name or position doesn't necessarily mean they will be a good reference. Name-dropping someone you believe to be of influence also doesn't work if the receiver has no idea who that person is. The person whose name you drop needs to know your *skills*, not just like you as a person. If the employer is asking questions about your work habits and your reference is unable to answer, chances are you will not get the job.

Who you know can help with your network, and there are probably some industries that still operate in this manner, but using connections is not a surefire method. Generally, you should rely on what you know, how you perform, and your work ethic. Networking may alert you to the opportunity, get your foot in the door, and put your name forward when it otherwise may not have been noticed, but it is still up to you to make the impression.

SOCIAL MEDIA

Social media can be your friend or your enemy. The new social norm is to post something every minute of your life. This might be an acceptable activity when you are sixteen, but when you get a bit older, you realize this could have repercussions in the job world. Prospective employers will look up a potential employee to see what their social media habits are; remember, once a picture or a post is out in cyberspace, it is there forever.

If you have published work, provided a review for someone else's writing, or joined a respectable association, social media will be to your advantage professionally. Posting political rants, inappropriate comments, or pictures about your personal misadventures does not make you look like a stable person. I understand you have the right to live your life and post or share whatever you want. However, be selective with your posts and limit public exposure of private matters to close friends.

Although rare, I have heard of potential employers ask for passwords to these accounts. That is an invasion of privacy. If you are asked for your passwords, you probably don't want to work there anyway. Chances are this kind of company will be monitoring your every move, making it a very uncomfortable workplace.

Keep a clean social profile. Advertising for employees has expanded beyond the newspaper and physical job postings. Companies are now using social media to advertise their need for employees. Using your profile, you can subscribe to these channels to quickly receive job notices. You do not want prospective employers noticing your previous night's drunk ramblings.

KEEP YOUR ONLINE PERSONA PROFESSIONAL.

Your online image is something you can control and use to your advantage. Again, you are fully entitled to your life, opinions, and activities. But companies also have a reputation they want to maintain. They don't want any kind of scandal to be connected to them by way of your activities.

CURRENT JOB AND SOCIAL MEDIA

The most critical no-no is posting negative statements about your current employer, especially with a public profile. Or worse yet, when you are socially connected with your coworkers—posting negative opinions while at work just makes it that much worse. You may think, *How will anyone know?* Everything you post has a date stamp. If anyone bothered to stop and check, they would know you are posting on social media instead of working. Slamming your current place of work does not demonstrate any kind of loyalty to the company. Anyone can look up your posts to gauge your opinions or feelings about your place of work.

If your current employer is looking to downsize, the most likely candidate for dismissal could be the disgruntled employee posting negatively about work *during* work hours. Why advertise the fact that you hate your job? It probably will not help your case if your posts mention that you are looking for another job. Spreading the word on social media will invariably get back to your current boss. Not to mention, potential employers can access public posts, and if you disparage your current employer, they may feel that you have no loyalty. Even if they want to hire you, disloyalty to an employer (even a competitor of theirs) is a red flag. They may ask themselves if you'll do the same thing to them if they hire you.

Loyalty to your current employer engenders a trusting relationship. If employers feel as though you would stab them in the back the second you don't like something, they will be less likely to offer you a job with their company.

SOCIAL MEDIA IS NOT A JOB CRITERION

When seeking a job, one of your criterion for acceptance should not be access to social media. For some reason, today's job hunters seem to think being disconnected from their social media account for longer than a half hour is the end of the world. Your account will still be there when the work is over. Asking a potential employer if you can use social media during work time isn't going to earn you any points, especially before you even have the job; it will raise suspicion that you won't be working while at work. When employed, your time is bought and paid for by the employer. This does not preclude you from checking your accounts on your lunch break; it's just usually frowned upon during work time.

When in the job interview, the most important aspect is that you want to work. A company will hire someone slightly less qualified but willing to work over someone qualified who doesn't want to put in the work or gives the impression of wanting to surf the internet while on the job.

PREPARING FOR THE INTERVIEW

Some say there is no way to prepare for an interview because you can never be sure what people will ask. While this may be partially true, there are standard go-to questions for many interviewers. There are also basics to prepare for. In a professional job interview, you will usually be asked to provide an overview of you, your past work experience, your education, and the benefits of hiring you. Unless you are a narcissist, this is harder than you think. Many people find it difficult to espouse their virtues; it generally just isn't in our DNA.

To be prepared, you need to understand yourself. What do you bring to the table? Thinking about your positive attributes is a start to preparing for an interview—in any industry. Part of your preparation can be positive self-talk and making a list of why someone should hire you. Maybe talk with a friend or close work colleague to help you identify the strengths of *you*. This is also where your family can help you focus on the positives you bring to the workplace.

WHAT SKILLS DO YOU HAVE?

Other people have just as many skills as you do. Consider the sheer volume of people applying for a single job. Sometimes there are hundreds of applicants for one job. When this happens, potential employers can afford to pick and choose who they want to represent their company. You need to stand out by demonstrating the skills you have that others don't. Emphasize your skills that match those within the job advertisement, selling those skills to the potential employer, convincing them you are the right person for the job. Provide an overview of your past employment and demonstrate how you completed those tasks with the skills you have that no one else has. And if you don't have precisely every skill they require, identify your transferable skills—the experience you have that is similar in nature to what is requested and can be easily adapted to the job advertisement.

Your résumé and your examples must match. Use both your résumé and your interview to tell the story of you. If this is the only opportunity you have to win the job, you need to make sure the potential employer has your full story—without providing unnecessary details. Think about all the skills you have in a positive light and draw a chart if you need to, mapping your skills with what the job requirements are.

WHAT TO BRING WITH YOU

Some feel they shouldn't bring anything with them to an interview. However, those who walk in with nothing—no paper, no pen, and no documents—scream lack of interest. You should bring a copy of the job advertisement with you; this can help keep you on track with what the potential employer is looking for in an employee. Bring a copy of your résumé. This may sound strange, but if you're nervous, you may not remember what you wrote. If you have customized your résumé for the different jobs you are applying for, you will need a reminder of what skills you provided for this particular job.

If the interviewer asks for proof of your education, bring copies. More often than you would think, people stretch the truth on their résumé in the hopes of getting their foot in the door for either an interview or a job; these days, you have to prove you have the education you say you do. Bring your references in a separate document.

Some people include references in their résumé as they are applying, but this can be presumptuous. The problem is you have just shared someone else's personal information, and just because you used them once does not mean they will always be willing to be your reference. Your references should be updated as often as you apply for a job, and you should also check with your references each time you use them.

You can also bring a cheat sheet with you—a bulleted list of the skills, projects, or initiatives you have taken part in. It doesn't mean you read from the sheet word for word; it is meant to jog your memory, outline the skill sets that you have, and display what sets you apart from the competition. Sometimes you are your own worst critic; ask a friend or colleague for help or advice on your accomplishments. It may be a short conversation where you brainstorm the different projects you worked on together, but it will help with the nerves and remembering what qualifies you to do the job.

HOW TO PREPARE

Not only should you speak about your own experience, but some companies expect you to have a high-level understanding of what the company you are applying for does. Do some research. Read up on the company you want to work for. What do they do, what are their values, and what kind of employees already work there?

Research on the company isn't always easy. Some companies have great websites and are a good source of information; for others, you may have to dig deeper. If you know someone who works at the company, tap into their knowledge. Ask questions about the position if you can. If you know someone who works in a specific area where you want to work, have a conversation with them. If you know the hiring person, there is no harm in speaking with them before applying for the job, giving you a sense of whether or not you're ready for the change or if the job is more extensive than the ad stated.

Make sure you get your facts right. It will seem very odd if the information you give to the interviewer is incorrect. Interviewers can tell when you have done the research, but it does not provide a good impression if you attribute work to this company that they never completed.

Bottom line, be prepared to talk about yourself, what makes you the person for the job, and why you will be a good fit at the company. Research the company and connect their end goals with your own. Be specific and come prepared.

THE INTERVIEW

The interview is the standard by which most people decide whether they want to hire someone. In some sense, you will never be ready for every potential question—again, there's no crystal ball. But you can set yourself up for success in other ways.

BE ON TIME

You can prepare all you want, having all your documentation and samples of work prepared in advance. You can be ready to go and nail all those questions perfectly. However, if you are late for the interview, you have most likely sealed your fate. The interviewer has probably set up interview times for more than just you. If you are late, that throws the entire schedule off and could impact others. You have therefore made a very poor impression.

Leave for the interview early, especially if you don't know where the interview is or are concerned about finding parking. Ensure you have time for any unforeseen challenges or delays. Although there may be a legitimate reason for being late (i.e., "My car broke down"), chances are this person interviewing you does not know you or your habits. They are judging you based on what they see or know. If, for example, your car does break down, then you should have a phone number to let someone know what happened.

Most people are pretty understanding; life happens. However, if you show up looking like you survived a hard night of partying, or you just rolled out of bed, the excuse is going to sound similar to "The dog ate my homework." Showing up late, in the employer's eyes, is a possible indication of tardiness as an employee. This could make or break your chances of getting hired.

REVIEW OF EDUCATION

You will be asked to explain your level of education—your *relevant* education. Nobody cares if you took a basket-weaving course. Speak to any degrees, certificates, diplomas, or extra credit courses pertinent to the job.

Education, whether directly related or not, could qualify you for the job. This is where transferable skills from education come into play. Although your education may not be directly applicable, your area of study might be close enough to the job. A degree states that you can be taught and you can learn.

What does not help is taking half a degree and then stating on your résumé that you have a full degree. That's lying. If you started the degree program or are currently still enrolled, say that, but also have a plan to finish said program. Even being in a program demonstrates a willingness to educate yourself, build your skill set, and, more importantly, a desire to learn. Going to school while also working or wanting to work suggests you have no problem with hard work.

You might be asked to prove your education. If you state you have a certain degree, you better be able to substantiate it, even if your education is not relevant to the job. Anyone could say that they are a rocket scientist. If a potential employer figures out you're lying, it won't matter how impressive the lie is.

REVIEW OF EXPERIENCE

Reviewing your experience is a tricky question. Each potential employer expects something different. Some prefer to hear only about directly relatable experiences. Most people don't always have precisely applicable expertise to share. Many of us rely on past work experience to fill the void and highlight our skills. Some employers simply want to know about the things you can do. They may be looking for someone to fill a gap in their current team. If they need a specific, obscure skill set demonstrated in your work history, it might be your lucky day. However, be careful not to go off on a rambling tangent filled with jumbled words that are no longer fully connected to the question asked. If the people across the table from you start looking bored, wrap up your thought and be done.

Be thorough but concise in your explanation, as this is your opportunity to sell yourself. Relate your skills to the original job advertisement. (Just because you know how to take a picture does not mean you are a photographer, for instance.)

GIVE EXAMPLES

Always provide examples. It does you no good to state you can do something without the evidence to back it up. If your résumé states that you've written various documents, be prepared to answer what kind. If your answer is "I wrote an email once for my boss," you are not a writer. However, if you state that you have written reports and a wide assortment of correspondence, you need to provide specific examples. You could say, "I have written technical reports in layman's terms, to explain our financial position to our board of directors." You have now supported the claim that you can write. If these documents are publicly available (as in, you wouldn't be sharing confidential information from your past job), sharing examples of your work can prove helpful in acquiring a job.

If you can't think of direct examples, you will struggle, mainly because you are nervous. Tell a story of a situation you were in and how you solved the problem. This will provide a better description of what you can do, how you can communicate, and how you can relate ideas. Using storytelling offers context to the person interviewing you. Put yourself in the hiring manager's shoes. If they are unfamiliar with the past job you are using as an example of your work, you will need to provide background and context for them to understand the role you played.

Provide the relevant details but, again, always be concise. You don't want to take too much time but just enough that you have painted a complete picture of your skills. Don't state details like "It was a Tuesday at 3:23 p.m., and it was raining." That's unnecessary information. Just present facts that are connected to the question that was asked. If you don't have work experiences to share as examples, use non-work stories. You can use examples from volunteer work or home life, really anything that demonstrates you have the skill that the employer is looking for.

WHY DID YOU LEAVE YOUR LAST JOB?

To answer why you are leaving your current job (or the one you had previously), don't say, "Because my boss is a tool." Or that your coworkers are out to get you. Or the workplace is a cesspool of nepotism. Even if all those things are true, don't say them. Stating these sentiments will just label you as a troublemaker or someone difficult to work with. Although technically you are honest, this kind of honesty won't do you any favours in the end. Don't bash the company you left or want to leave. This is called *burning bridges to the ground.*

If you plan to leave or are exploring options, speak highly of the company you plan to leave, as this will help you with your future network or possibly even a reference. Whether you had an excellent overall experience or not, you should try to find something positive about your former employment place. If the idea of praising the "living hell" of your last job sounds daunting, focus your energy on one aspect that was positive. Even a bad experience can bring about some positives.

There are many ways to explain why you want to leave your current job. Frame your response in a positive light. Your answer can include goals such as personal development, building your skill set, or growth opportunities that may be available elsewhere. You may also like the values of the company where you are applying to work or the product the company develops. You can also state that if this job hadn't come up, you wouldn't be leaving your current position; if this is your dream job, state that. This answer could display the passion you have for working for the company.

WHY DO YOU WANT TO WORK HERE?

The answer to "Why do you want to work here?" should be similar to your explanation for leaving your previous job. This is another opportunity to demonstrate what you know about the company with whom you are interviewing. Again, if this is your dream job, state that fact. Anything positive you found in your research should be referenced. If this is an entry-level position, it might be appropriate to mention your opportunity for growth. Acknowledge that you are starting your career but want to learn, grow, and contribute to the larger whole of the company.

Regardless of what level you are applying for, you want to add value and contribute to the company's goals. Whether it's true or not, it's never appropriate to mention that you plan to take over the company (or that you think the rest of the employees are idiots who couldn't find their way out of a wet paper bag). Be respectful and focus on yourself and why you want to work there. Don't point fingers or insert subtle jabs at your last place of work.

KEEP YOUR ANSWERS RELEVANT

With any question asked during the interview, keep your answers relevant to the potential job opportunity and the question. Providing irrelevant (albeit interesting) information that isn't connected to the question will not demonstrate your knowledge; rather, it might just broadcast that you like to talk. Fully answer the question, without oversharing or rambling. It's okay to be nervous or excited—interviewers take nerves into account, and they know this can be a stressful experience—but bring the conversation back to relevant information if you are prattling.

There is also such a thing as not saying enough. If the interviewer has to ask the same question in several different ways to get an answer, or if there are several follow-up questions, you are either not understanding the question or not providing the interviewer with the information they are looking for. Instead of just fumbling through, state that you don't understand. Or you can paraphrase the question back to the interviewer to confirm your understanding of the question. You can also just take a moment to collect your thoughts. Try not to feel pressured into blurting out an answer. A thought-out response that takes a few seconds longer is better than blurting out nonsense.

ASK QUESTIONS

There is no need to ask questions for the sake of asking. If you ask something silly like, "What's the vacation policy?" then you would have been better off not saying anything at all. You should be reviewing the job advertisement and highlighting the items that are not clear or the responsibilities you would like more

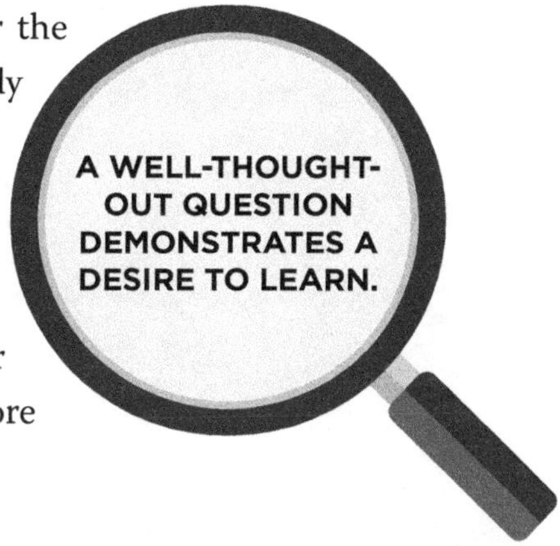

information about. Sometimes these items are covered during an overview of the job or over the course of the interview. If not, there is usually an opportunity for you to ask the interviewer.

Asking questions demonstrates your ability to think and inquire. There is no need to fill dead space with inane comments or questions. If you feel you must ask a question, ask about the successful candidate's expectations within the first thirty, sixty, and ninety days. This type of question will give you a good indication of your learning curve if you are offered the job. You could also use this opportunity to go back to questions you may have stumbled on or that need more detail. For example, you could say, "I don't feel I fully answered your last question. Could I provide some additional clarity?" There are very few people who would decline that request. Using your time to provide more information shows maturity and awareness that you may need to correct or update something that you said.

SKILLS—WHAT YOU CAN DO

All too often, résumés simply list places the applicant has worked. While important, it's more important to describe what you did at those jobs. An employer wants to know what tasks you performed, what decisions you made, what you can do that matches what they need, what you can do that no one else can, and what you know how to do. Don't only give a list of activities. Match it up to the place you worked, and make sure you can substantiate your claim.

You may need to provide a demonstration or examples of your skills. Your résumé is the first step in demonstrating that you are the right candidate for the job. The hiring manager knows what they want in an employee, but they want to know what you can do, not what you think they want to hear. Repeating the job posting does not demonstrate that you understand the job requirements—it indicates that you can memorize. You do yourself a disservice if you think this is the best way to get a job. Most potential employers can see through a simple recitation of their job description. If you successfully win the job, you need to deliver on what you claim you can do. What will happen if you get the job but lied during the interview? If you can't produce the skills you claimed to have, you may be shown the door in short order.

No matter what job you are applying for, there are common themes that employers are looking for. These skills or behaviours are pretty much universal to every type of job. Essentially, your potential employer wants to know if you can function independently. They want someone they don't have to watch over twenty-four seven. They want people who can follow vague instructions and still achieve the intended outcome and won't empty the vault if left to their own devices.

MULTITASKING IS NOT A SKILL

Multitasking means being able to do more than one task at a time—which, technically, isn't possible. When someone says they are a multitasker, they usually do many things haphazardly, with no single task done precisely. If you say, "I can talk on the phone and write an email," this tells the future employer you only give half your attention to a task at any given time. The true meaning of a multitasker, in a work setting, is having more than one project operating at a time, while assuring the necessary tasks are completed within the scope of work initially outlined.

Doing one project at a time is not efficient. Sometimes there are lags in some of your tasks, which means filling the lag time with something else that needs doing. If you are waiting for information, you can get started on the next bit of work that needs your attention. Or, if you have received information that you were previously waiting for, you can finish that bit of work. Essentially you are guaranteeing that you can account for and fill your time during the workday. Sitting and doing nothing while you are waiting for direction or information is not productive.

UNDERSTANDING WRITTEN AND ORAL INSTRUCTIONS

Understanding written instructions means you can read a document and discern your role or what portions are your responsibility. I once had a boss who scribbled notes on a scrap piece of paper, and I had to figure out what he wanted me to do. Written instructions can be very concise and detailed instructions of your task or project. Or it can be very vague and high-level notes (or even diagrams) of the expected work. The point is that, as an employee, you need to be able to discern the expectation of the task given to you via written document no matter the document's format.

Oral instruction typically refers to quick instructions, sometimes given by your boss as they run out the door. Are you able to figure out what those instructions meant? Essentially, you should be able to get 90 percent of the requested task done with minimal direction. Remember, there may not always be someone around to ask. You may have to use your brain and powers of deduction to figure out what needs to be done. Before an interview, prepare an example of when you have achieved this in the past. The best example would be to describe a specific situation where you had minimal information and how you went about finding the details you needed to complete the task. Include the steps you took to find information and any inventive channels you used to assist in your search. Note if you were able to ask questions or not and with whom you spoke to for more details. Finally, outline the outcome and how successful (or even unsuccessful) you were. Even if you were unsuccessful, you should take away some lessons to apply to the next situation. If you can articulate an ability to learn through hardships, you've just earned some points with whoever is interviewing you.

Understanding written and oral instructions means you are able to figure out what needs to be done without someone walking you through every step in the process. Providing the hiring manager examples of your ability to figure things out for yourself demonstrates that you have this critical skill in the workforce.

WORK AS A TEAM

Sometimes it's not all about you. Sometimes you need to assist your coworkers to achieve goals, and vice versa. You may not have all the necessary skills to accomplish your assigned tasks. That's where a reliable team comes in.

As you apply for a job or are interviewed for the position, talk about working as a team and the positive results your team achieved. While important, explaining only your accomplishments does not demonstrate how you can share the limelight. Show that you know how to share the work and accolades. Demonstrate the recognition that more people involved can create a better product in the end, showing employers that you recognize the benefit of others' perspectives. Be humble and acknowledge there are many things you don't know but others do, which is why working as a team is an important skill.

Sure, describe your personal, individual accomplishments, but chances are, your most significant successes involved a team. The chance that you have accomplished a significant project or task independently and without input or assistance from others is slim to none. Acknowledge the work of others while outlining your role. Understanding the overall success demonstrates an overarching knowledge of the entire project and an ability to recognize the importance of tasks that aren't your own.

WORK WITH MINIMAL DIRECTION (A.K.A. A PROBLEM SOLVER)

At times you will be assigned a task, and your boss will leave you to your own devices. They might be in meetings, away from the office, or simply inaccessible. They've given you a task with minimal direction or instruction with only half of the information you need. Maybe they don't quite know what needs to be done and they expect you to figure it out. You need to be able to work without clear information; this is where the problem-solving part of your brain needs to start working. Don't kid yourself into thinking this doesn't happen often. It happens more often than receiving explicit instruction. At the end of the day, your boss doesn't usually care how you get there; they simply want what's been requested. And sometimes you need to tell them what is needed.

During the interview, you need to demonstrate how you can or have accomplished this in past work environments. Simply replying that you can do it doesn't really tell the potential employer anything. It may imply that you have always had everything laid out nice and neat for you or never had the opportunity to think on your own. Make sure you have an example or a story to illustrate how you have accomplished this skill in the past. Provide the full story of what you received for instruction, the gaps, and how you filled the gaps. A full range of problems you have solved, from big to small, will help paint the picture of what you can do with minimal information or direction.

TRANSFERABLE SKILLS

The words *transferable skills* are a bit murky in their translation. Sometimes it's interpreted as a specific skill set employers are looking for. Other times, it's a similar set of skills; you might require a bit of coaching but know the basics.

Some transferable skills include

- Data analysis—data is data, no matter what kind it is.
- Supervisory—this doesn't change from job to job; you are still dealing with people.
- Typing and data entry—again, this is the same skill and can be used anywhere you go.
- Research—it doesn't matter what you research; the skills are generally the same in any job.
- Problem-solving—a universal requirement, basically, assessing whether you can use your intelligence and experience to develop a solution to the problem in front of you. It doesn't matter where you go; there are always problems to solve.

- Various computer programs—there will always be proprietary or new software in this technological age, but it's important to keep up with the basic ones.

The more transferable skills you have, the better potential candidate you are. Transferable skills demonstrate your ability to learn and the ability to apply past learnings to new situations. Employers do not want to have to train every hire on everything. It's faster and easier to get someone up to speed if they are already familiar with the basic skills and tasks. Employers want people who are going to start delivering results sooner rather than later.

INTERVIEW TYPES

Most people believe there is only one kind of interview. You sit down with one person, or sometimes several, and they ask questions, you answer questions, and you've finished the interview. While this is the standard method of assessing potential employees, this is only one way for employers to hire.

Employers need someone who is going to fulfill the tasks required to make their business run. They will use every tool at their disposal to hire the best possible person for the job. If this means grilling every applicant with extra questions and assessments, they will. Hiring the wrong person costs companies a lot of money. This cost includes dollars to advertise the job, time to set up the new hire in the workplace and train them, effort to do so, and the loss of productivity that comes naturally with a new employee. Employers do their best to hire the person who is going to fulfill the work required of them. Most cannot afford to be slack in this area. It uses a lot of resources if they don't get it right the first time.

THE STANDARD

An employer asks the potential candidate questions in a standard interview. It doesn't get any more complicated than that. There is usually a set number of questions for every candidate—standard questions to provide an equal analysis of each potential employee. The point is to measure all candidates equally. The flaw in this is that each person is unique and will answer questions in a unique manner. So, really, the score given to each candidate is based on the preference and perspective of the person conducting the interview. In the absence of something more tangible or equitable, this is what people rely upon.

In some industries, the process is more relaxed, and the response of the interviewer is simply "I like you; you're hired." Other companies have to provide supporting evidence that the person selected is the best person for the job, requiring loads of documentation, processing, and possible hoops to jump through to get the person they feel can succeed in the position. Standard interviews can vary between business types and industry. You may be asked technical questions particular to individual tasks that occur on the job. Others might assume that you know the technical stuff and focus on the softer side of work because you are in the industry. It is also very possible there will be set questions but the person doing the interview deviates from those questions. Personal preference and personal style of the interviewer cannot be prepared for ahead of time.

THE CASUAL

Some industries are much more relaxed in their hiring practices. They have no standard set of questions, and every interview might be different. The employer may simply have a conversation with the potential candidate, and if they click over common interests, they could be hired. This conversation could be relatively short, only lasting a few minutes. If this is the case, you better bring your A game. You only have a limited window of time to make a good impression. You and the employer may bond over a love of fantasy fiction and develop a good relationship on the spot. Or, on the flip side, maybe the employer didn't like the way you shook hands and instantly disliked you.

As this is so casual, there isn't much you can prepare for; however, you can still be professional. These types of interviews could also be on the spot. You may be cold-calling and the hiring manager happens to be available and looking for staff. There is always a possibility that the manager has time to talk at the very moment you drop off your résumé. In this sense, be prepared at all times for a potential interview.

GOOD COP, BAD COP

There are times when two people interview might you. Sometimes one will be nice, and the other, not so much—essentially, a good cop, bad cop scenario. The purpose is to keep the candidate off balance. This situation tests the candidate's knowledge, assessing how they react to varying situations. It may appear that one interviewer is an ally, but in reality, they are setting up their counterpart to provoke you.

The key is not to react too strongly. Keep your cool and answer any questions openly, honestly, and as forthright as you can. Even though you may be provoked, keep a level head and be as respectful as possible. The test here is to see how you react under duress. There usually isn't a safety net if you are put on the spot in a real-life job. You will probably pass this test if you can keep your thoughts together and show some backbone while being professional.

HOSTILE

You may find yourself in a rare situation—a hostile interview. In these scenarios, the interviewer is deliberately trying to cause stress to see how you react in certain stressful situations. Usually, this type of interview is reserved for high-level executives, not for an entry-level position. It's a test of how you handle several issues at once while in the spotlight, when something goes sideways in the business you are responsible for. This type of interview could also be considered a test of your emotional intelligence. Do you keep your cool when faced with stressors, or do you lose your mind? It allows the interviewer to see how much of a poker face you have or whether your emotions are written all over your face.

It's not intended to address technical skills but rather to test your fortitude. How well you respond will determine your success. Understanding the process and its purpose will help you answer questions confidently. If you blow your top at the first hard or aggressive question, you've already lost the job.

THE SECOND INTERVIEW

Sometimes a decision on a candidate is not always black and white. When the employer interviews many people, they often need a second round to make a decision. After a while, all the candidates start to blend, and it is hard to distinguish one from the other. The second interview could be another test or assessment regarding whether or not you seem to fit in with the company. There are many directions this second round could take.

The second interview could simply be a repeat of the first interview, with the same people, and possibly even with the same questions. Sometimes the interviewer simply wants to refresh their memory of your answers or their impression of you.

There could be different people in the room. Maybe the interviewer wants someone else to weigh in on the decision and provide another opinion or perspective. Or it could be a different style of interview. Maybe your first interview was pretty tame, leaning towards a more standard type. The second interview may be more intense, another test of how well you would do on the job.

There could be more than one style of interview used in the second meeting, a combination of formal or informal. Formal would be in a boardroom with set parameters and someone taking notes. Or, it could be informal, merely a conversation. Maybe the interviewer wants to test how you do in the work environment. They just want a chat to firm up their decision that you are the right candidate for the job. You may also need to come in to work alongside someone, giving the employer the opportunity to assess your abilities and you the opportunity to review the work you'd be doing. They may or may not pay you for your time, but if they don't see potential to learn, you probably won't get the job.

One of the more challenging types of second interviews is meeting the team. You've passed all the other assessments, and the potential employer has narrowed the selection down to two or three people. The last test is figuring out if you can work with the rest of the team members. You now need to impress the people you could be working with, and this is a test of likeability—they either like you or they don't. An employer usually wants a harmonious work environment, and they don't want a new person coming in and messing that up. This test could make or break you in the job competition. If the team doesn't like you, it won't matter if you aced all the other assessments; you could be out of the running.

THE FOLLOW-UP

There are different schools of thought about following up on an application's status or after an interview. Some advocate following up with a thank-you note to the interviewers. You could follow up with an email or a phone call or simply drop off a message. Some potential employers may feel that it demonstrates a willingness to work and a genuine interest in the job. Others simply find the practice annoying. Receiving an email after an interview, in most instances, feels very superficial and disingenuous—most sound as though the sentiment is forced. A genuine thank-you at the end of an interview will serve you better.

AFTER AN APPLICATION

Applying for a job used to involve real interaction between the job seeker and the person hiring. People's interactions have diminished, much of the process taking place online. There is no opportunity to make a connection with the person reviewing the applications. This is why your résumé needs to stand out and why it's a good idea to follow up in person when possible. It depends on the type of business you are applying to, as there may not be an identifiable individual you can contact.

Following up on an application is probably more important than following up after an interview. With hundreds of applications to review, the process is not always easy, and employers don't want to sift through application after application. We have already talked about making your résumé stand out; now, you need to stand out. Checking in with the potential employer will leave an impression. However, you'll be quick to remove yourself from the running if you're rude in any way.

Instead of demanding to know when the interview or hiring will occur, say something like, "I applied for a job with your company a few weeks ago and am still interested in the position. I am wondering when interviews will be scheduled." Don't back the employer into a corner by making demands or suggesting you are perfect for the position. You might find yourself on the defensive when the potential employer demands you prove it. Be respectful of the employer's time and demonstrate a genuine interest in working for the company.

AFTER AN INTERVIEW

If you are genuinely appreciative at the end of the interview, there is no need to fill up the interviewer's inbox with another email or take up their time with a phone call. The only reason to follow up would be to provide additional information or documents requested during the interview, at which time you could further express gratitude for their time. If the employer has asked for references after the fact or a copy of your education documents, you could include additional comments. But keep it brief. Ten minutes after the interview, a separate note makes it seem like you are trying too hard to impress.

Don't misunderstand; some potential employers like their ego stroked in that manner. But many will see a thank-you note for what it is—very superficial, with no real sentiment behind the intent. After the interview, many notes tend to say the same thing, quoting the job advertisement, full of empty platitudes. If you are going to follow up with a message, be genuine and sure that the person receiving the note will appreciate the effort.

BEHAVIOUR

Just because you applied for a job does not guarantee the job is yours. Life is not fair, nor does life owe you anything. Just because you have been with a company for an extended period does not mean you automatically get that promotion or position you think you deserve. Loyalty to a company does not equal advancement. Most employers are looking for people who put effort into their careers. They do not want people who have a sense of entitlement. Employers want to see that you are serious about wanting to work for them. They want to see progressive experience within your résumé. They want to see continuous education, extra courses, seminars, anything that appears as if you want to expand your knowledge and are willing to develop your skills.

When you get rejected for a job (and you will get rejected), it is better to accept that decision with dignity and professionalism. Throwing a temper tantrum does not win you any points, and you want to keep doors open for future opportunities. Maybe there is not a position that fits you right now, but there might be in the future. You need to leave a good impression, even in the face of a rejection.

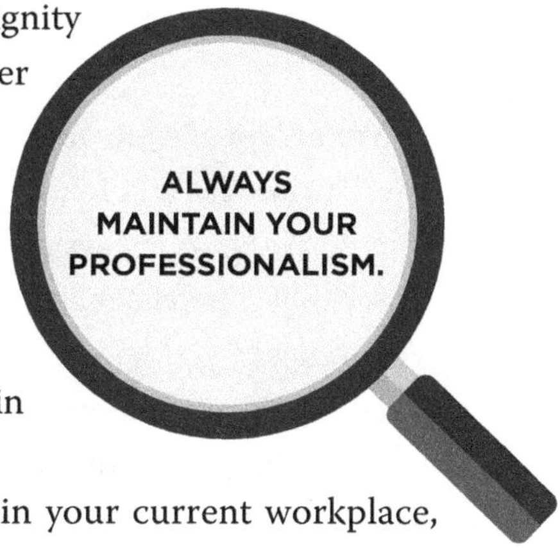

If you apply for a promotion within your current workplace, how you conduct yourself is even more critical. Remember, gossip spreads like wildfire. If you are bitching and moaning to anyone who will listen about not getting a job, that behaviour will come back to haunt you. Crying to someone doesn't help your chances; it merely reinforces the employer's decision not to hire you.

After an interview, in the case where you did not get the job, ask the hiring manager for an interview debrief. An interview debrief is where you can ask how you can improve on your interview skills, receiving honest feedback. This action demonstrates professional behaviour and a willingness to learn. The conversation between you and the employer will be much more casual as the interview's tension will no longer be there. You will have a much more open discussion about where you need to improve. Having an open conversation about your interview could open future opportunities with the same company. You could also talk about other skills or experiences you might need to succeed in the future. This will provide you an opportunity to learn, improving your chances for the next interview.

There is also the genuine possibility that you may meet the same hiring manager in another interview with this company, thus demonstrating that you can learn from your previous interview experience. Having an open conversation and demonstrating the ability to learn and grow will positively impact a potential employer.

EXPECTATIONS

You've accepted a job offer, and you are about to experience your first day. During the first few days or the first week, someone is assigned to help you out, always answering questions or providing support. This can feel excellent and easy at times, but it doesn't last very long. Very quickly, you will be expected to do the job for which you were hired. To be frank, after the glow wears off, new jobs usually become more challenging. You are not going to know everything you need to know. You aren't going to understand the ins and outs of this new work environment.

There will be unfamiliar company processes and policies. Expect to make mistakes—a lot of them. Again, it takes a good year to be effective at your job. It takes a year or more to fully understand your position and how everyone else's jobs interact with yours. Then you need to learn and understand how to fit into the workplace culture. Not only do you need to know these things, but you also need to learn the practical items. How do you get paid? How do you ask for time off? What happens when you are sick? Where do you park? The list goes on. There is so much you don't know. Don't fool yourself into thinking you know everything about the company. It's easier on you and those around you if you admit you don't know something and ask for help. Sometimes just asking will save you a lot of problems.

SEEKING A PROMOTION

If you have accepted a job with the expectation that you will be promoted shortly after your hire, you may need to revise your thoughts, especially if you are in an entry-level position. Many people employed by that company have been there significantly longer than you have. If length of employment is the main criteria for promotion, you are in last place. It always depends on what job is available, your skills, the company's hiring policies, and how they view loyalty.

If you have accepted a position with the mindset that this is a short-term deal, this job may not be for you. If you think you are deserving of an immediate promotion just because you are you, you aren't going to make any friends or win points with the boss. You should enter any job with the determination to your best work no matter what the job. This "temporary" job could turn out to be the best job you've ever had and could become the permanent solution to your job hunt. Temper your expectations as you accept and begin the new-job journey.

THE SCREENING

Employers need criteria to screen potential employees. While some intuition is involved in a hiring decision, most employers select future employees using quantitative methods. Generally speaking, gut or intuition is the last piece of qualitative data used to make a final decision. A good employer will attempt to develop some standardized method to validate the hiring decision they are trying to make. Some will use one single tried-and-true method that works for them. Others will have a human resources department providing criteria to select the best candidate for the job. Sometimes employers will use a computer application to assist in the screening.

In every case, there is a human being doing some or all of the applicant's screening; this is when subjectivity is a factor in the selection process. As mentioned, you need to make an excellent first impression, starting with your résumé or, if you can, in person. This will decide whether or not you move through the hiring process. With the volume of résumés that an employer sees, yours will be quickly set aside if there are red flags. You might be screened out before even being considered if there's a bad first impression of your résumé. It cannot be stressed enough that you need to put every effort into making yourself stand out. Remember, several hundred other people are vying for the same job. Some are much more experienced than you are—not to be discouraging, but this is a fact you need to recognize going into the job hunt.

TESTING

You might have to undergo some testing before you ever make it to the interview stage. This is another form of screening the candidates. With a quick turnover of employees, employers do not want to waste time with a so-so candidate who costs time and money to get them to do the job they were hired for. Employers want people who can come in and do the job with little hand-holding. Do not blow off these tests. If you don't do the tests or don't respond, you have just made the potential employer's job much more manageable by making the list of candidates smaller. If you keep applying at the same company and don't complete the tests, you could be labelled negatively; pretty soon, you will automatically be in the NO pile.

Tests include personality tests, analysis tests, and simple typing tests. Tests can be administered before an interview or after the interview. The pressure of being surprised by something you were not expecting is also a test. Now, how will you perform? You might be provided with a subject matter and asked to prepare a presentation. Sometimes you will have very little time to prepare and present in front of a very critical crowd. The higher up you go, the more likely you will be exposed to more than an interview.

Put yourself in the potential employer's position. Are you going to gamble on a high-paid, senior position with only an interview? It would be in the employer's best interest to use every form of assessment to ensure they have the best person for the job.

PRE-SCREENING

Sometimes when you are submitting an application or résumé, you are asked a series of questions. These pre-screening questions are usually asking for confirmation of your skills. It may be tempting to lie (or stretch the truth), hoping you move forward to the next step. But as soon as someone looks at your résumé, it will be obvious you weren't truthful. If you lie through the pre-screen and are still somehow considered, it will most likely come out in the interview process. You aren't fooling anyone if you try to bluff your way through. Lies will always catch up to you. Your best bet is to be as honest as possible.

Some pre-screening is done completely via software applications, meaning a computer algorithm decides if your résumé makes it to an actual human being. As a hunter, consider using similar language to that used in the job advertisement. It's not likely that the employer will create additional metadata outside of what they have already written. The employer has written a thorough review of what they want in an employee. Take the time to make sure your résumé and cover letter reflect not only the skills that employers are looking for but also the language they are expecting. Sometimes this means a complete rewrite of your résumé and cover letter to match the language that the algorithm is expecting to find.

Pre-screening can also be done by a person at the company. Visualize this scenario: you are cold-calling and pounding the pavement, or whatever you want to call it. You walk into a business and see a receptionist. You ask if the company is hiring; the receptionist says that they are. Now you can do a few different things here. You can ask to leave your résumé, or you could ask if there is anyone available to speak with regarding the job. The receptionist may very well be the gatekeeper of the applicants, which means he or she may ask you a few questions. If they do take the résumé, make sure you are polite, respectful, and thorough if they ask questions. He or she will most likely tell the potential employer their impression of you. If you decline to answer, stating, "I will only speak to the person in charge of hiring," or are rude in any way, you have just pulled yourself out of the process.

Think of it this way: If you are successful, you will have to work with the receptionist whom you treated rudely. And that won't be a comfortable relationship in the future. This receptionist could be the very person who recommends you for an interview, so tread carefully.

OTHER SCREENING TACTICS

Other times, you may talk to someone as you hand in a résumé or application. Chances are, this person is sizing you up. They may not be the actual employer, but they may be a source the employer trusts. Take each of these opportunities to make a good impression. As you are job hunting, you never know when you will meet someone who can help you in your search. It doesn't matter if the person is the receptionist, the human resource manager, or the president of a major corporation; be respectful. Any one of those people can offer their opinion on your fit with the company you just applied to work for. Any opportunity could be a networking opportunity. One of these people could have a job opportunity in the future and recommend you—perhaps based solely on that initial meeting. All possibilities should be viewed as prescreening into (or possibly out of) a job.

Sometimes you may be asked for information or be required to go through a screening procedure. You may get a call; however, you could be contacted via email or text. Pay attention. If you come back with "I didn't see this" or "I was out of town," or any other similar excuse, it will most likely be seen in a negative light. Most people have their phone connected to their hand. It's no longer very likely that you missed seeing a request; rather, they will assume you probably didn't bother with the assignment. This is not a good look for you or your future opportunities.

THE COMPETITION

You may be a new graduate or someone who has been in the workforce for a significant period. But you are not the end-all or be-all of applicants. There is always someone out there who has *more* than you do. It could be education, experience, or a better network of contacts. Just because you feel you are the most qualified or right for a job does not mean the hiring company feels the same way.

When you graduate, when you enter the market, and the current state of the economy all affect your ability to find a job. If you have no experience during an economic downturn, it is improbable you will be hired into your dream job right out of the gate. Companies that can afford to hire in an economic recession will attract and hire the best of the best. They have little need to advertise—people will be knocking down their door. Chances for landing a job are better in a booming economy.

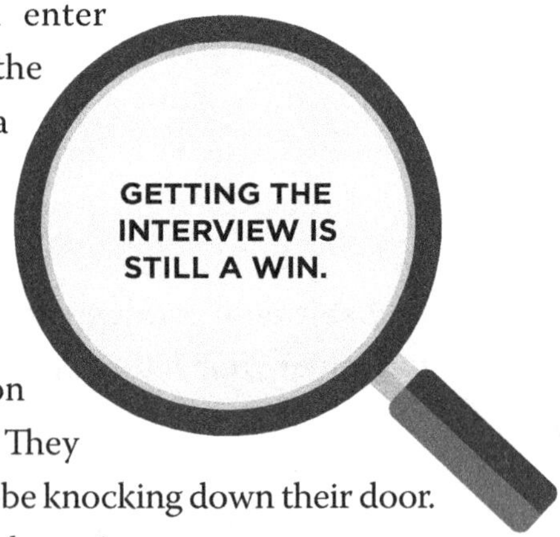

The reality is that sometimes employers just need someone to keep a chair warm and don't care who is working for them. But once you get your foot in the door, use that opportunity to shine; demonstrate what you can do when given a chance. You need to exude the confidence and knowledge that you are worth keeping around.

IT'S NOT YOU, IT'S THEM

Lack of success might not be about what you did wrong but about what other people did right. If you make it through the screening process and the interview but don't ultimately land the job, it may not have been something you did or said. There might be one thing that someone else did just a bit better than you. Maybe the other candidates had more experience than you, or their past work experience was an exact match to what the company needed. Perhaps they were more confident in their responses.

Making it to the interview means you did something right. Most people don't interview as a courtesy; that would waste valuable time. Consider how vast the workforce is compared to the available jobs, and then narrow that down to your specific industry; there is a lot of competition for jobs. Even if the competition has been narrowed down to four people for the same position, one of your competitors could have an exceptional day and nail the interview questions, while perhaps you stumble a bit. A minor factor could make or break your search for a job.

ACCEPTANCE

Many are under the misconception that they just need to impress the interviewer. This is not the case. They aren't just interviewing you; you are also interviewing them. Do they seem genuine? Do you feel a sense of comfort in speaking with these people? Do you think you could work in this business? Do you want to work there? If there is tension in the room, if the workplace atmosphere does not seem like something you can live with, you need to consider all those factors as well.

Your mindset is also something you need to take into consideration. What do you want to get out of this job? Is this a stepping-stone job? Is this a long-term job? Is this your dream job? Consider also what you may have heard about the company or what you found through your research. Is there a high turnover? Maybe this is the norm within the industry, or perhaps the environment is toxic. And you may not know the reason for a high turnover rate.

These observations can also prove positive. Do people rave about working here? Are there amazing perks for every employee? Does it sound like a great place to work?

YOU CAN SAY NO, TOO

If you are searching for a job, you may become desperate for any job. Your first instinct may be to say yes to a position without considering what you have said yes to. Just because you have gone through the entire process does not mean you have to say yes to a job offer. You can say no. Many people feel guilty for wasting a prospective employer's time and will simply say yes for that reason. But remember, you have been interviewing a potential employer too. If this job is not going to provide you with what you are looking for, you are better off saying no.

Saying no now will save both you and the employer problems in the future. Employers ultimately want a person who genuinely wants to be at their company, not someone taking the job out of obligation. As you go through the process and learn more about the position, perhaps you realize this is not the job you thought it was. In this case, saying no is probably in your best interest.

YOU CAN SAY YES, WITH CONDITIONS

A yes with conditions usually will only occur in higher-level positions. If you are applying for a job at a burger joint, then demanding certain work conditions will likely result in you being shown the door. These workplaces have stacks of people looking for a job; they don't need you.

Once you are at a certain point in your career, the pool of qualified applicants tends to become shallower with experience and education. While unreasonable demands, such as access to the company jet, may not fly, additional compensation might. You could negotiate the wage, the hours of work, or the allotted annual vacation. There are always items within the authority of the potential employer that you can negotiate. But, again, you must be reasonable with your requests. Just because the pool is shallow does not mean the company can't find someone else.

THIS JOB MIGHT NOT BE FOR YOU

Sometimes when you interview for a job, there is this niggling feeling in the back of your mind saying, "I don't think I want to work here."

That's your instinct telling you something is off about this workplace and accepting the job might be a mistake. You then need to make a hard decision. Do you suffer through a terrible work environment to gain a paycheck and experience, or do you say no and hope something else comes along? Consider your next job interview. You will need to explain why you left your prior job to the new interviewer. Accepting a job that you know you don't necessarily want could be a career-killing move.

I once entered a workplace for a job interview, and you could cut the tension in that room with a knife. Before I even sat down, I knew I didn't want to work in that kind of environment. I deliberately blew the interview to get out of there as fast as I could.

SIGNS YOU DON'T WANT TO WORK SOMEWHERE

Many signs speak to why you wouldn't want to work somewhere. Number one would be a high turnover. If you apply to work at a place you patronize and there are new people every other week, use that as a sign that the morale is low or that the working environment is toxic. If the business cannot keep staff, there is only one common denominator—the boss. The boss is probably a jerk that no one wants to work for, or maybe he or she treats the staff like garbage.

Ever walk into a workplace, and you could hear a pin drop? Have you ever walked by a work unit and noticed (or even been able to feel) the tension of the staff? These are red flags that this would not be a great place to work. Starting a new job is hard enough without having to deal with a lousy work environment. It's hard enough learning a new culture, let alone learning how to live with an autocratic boss or a grumpy coworker. There are most likely underlying causes for the tension, but you need to decide if you are willing to subject yourself to it.

When interviewing for a position, there are always opportunities to ask questions about the work environment and those who work at the company—but phrase the question appropriately. You can't ask if the boss is an ass, but you can ask what the company's values are and what culture the team embraces. You can also ask how information is communicated to staff. If the person interviewing doesn't want to answer those questions or can't answer it in a positive way, that's a red flag. If the interviewer skirts the question or deflects or stumbles through an explanation, they are probably hiding the truth about the work environment.

Perhaps your interviewer is disengaged or disgruntled and paints a gloomy picture. This is the first time you've met this person; if they dump this emotional baggage on you, that's a sign you don't want to work there. Even if the central issue isn't the work environment, do you want to work for this grumpy person? If the interviewer can't display a realistic idea of what you're getting yourself into in a positive way, trust your instincts and walk away.

REJECTION

The number of rejection letters you get will astound you. You will apply to more jobs than you can imagine. Many people receive stacks of letters thanking them for their time or application; all are politely saying "Thanks, but no thanks." My own stack of PFO ("please f**k off) letters could be considered a fire starter. As we discussed, this is not necessarily a knock against you. Some applicants sail through interviews but can't do the job once they get there—which just means that the job will be up for grabs again. You need to keep applying. Change your résumé or get coaching for your interview. Maybe you sounded like a bumbling fool during the interview or couldn't overcome nerves. You might need to develop techniques to calm your nerves as you answer the questions posed.

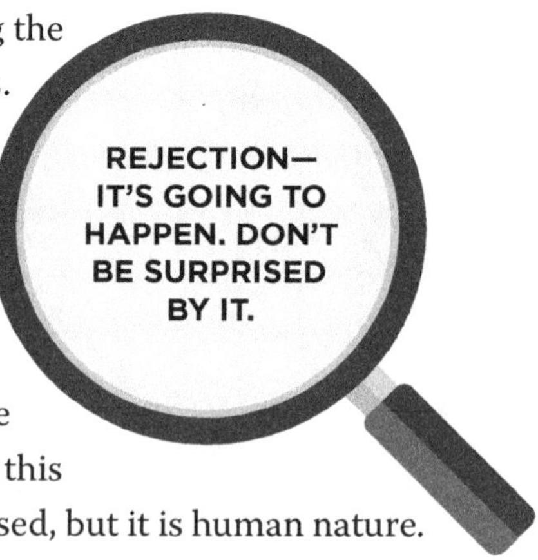

You might be rejected not for your skill set but for how you mesh with the interviewer. People generally hire those who are similar in personality to them; this is not discriminatory—perhaps a tad biased, but it is human nature. We surround ourselves with people who we can understand and relate to. People like easy relationships, not hard ones. Think of an introvert trying to understand how an extrovert thinks. That just makes the introvert tired.

Sometimes finding the right fit for both you and the employer takes time. So you were rejected from a job you felt you were the perfect fit for; in reality, beyond the job advertisement, you have no idea what the employer is looking for in an employee. Maybe you are applying for a promotion within a company you are currently a part of. The process remains the same. You still have to apply and compete for the position. Jobs are not handed out like free samples. You need to put the effort in to get a new job. You may even have a personal relationship with the person hiring, but this does not guarantee you a free ride—nor does this mean you know what the potential employer's expectations are.

Remember, working *for* someone and working *with* someone are very different things. Your résumé got you the interview; it is up to you to sell yourself after that.

YOU GOT THE JOB

Congratulations, you're hired! Now what? Now you have to face the realities of work. If this is your first job, you will have a steeper learning curve than those who are more experienced. If this is your first "adult" job, the reality is going to slap you in the face. This is nothing like the job you had in high school. If you are later in your career, none of this will come as much of a shock.

The first thing to remember is that the person hired better be the person who shows up to work. I want to share a story with you.

There was a young man in an interview. This young man wore a suit, and was clean cut and very neat in his appearance. During the interview, he described his job aspirations for the future and had a plan for the money he was going to earn that would help put him through post-secondary education. His earnest portrayal won him the job. Now, fast-forward to the following Monday. The employer asked where his new employee was and was directed towards someone he assumed to be a customer. This person turned out to be his new employee, who was wearing ripped jeans and a dirty T-shirt, with numerous piercings (which were obviously taken out for the interview). He looked, overall, like he had come to work after rolling around in the dirt. This was not the person who the employer had hired! Even his attitude was utterly different. He could not understand how his attire did not fit in this particular workplace, and he became belligerent about that fact.

You can wear whatever you'd like on your own time; when you are getting paid to do a job, you should toe the company line. There are expectations of appearance, attire, and attitude at every workplace. Sometimes, they are not always spelled out; however, common sense should tell you that being rude is just not acceptable.

YOU ARE THE NEW PERSON, REMEMBER THAT

There are a couple things to avoid when you start a new job. Your first question shouldn't be about vacation and how many breaks you get. That might not look like you came to *work*. Telling people how to do their job is also something to avoid as it might alienate you from coworkers you hope to get along with. Defer to those who have been there longer. This won't always be necessary, but it is the best way to learn the job. You will need someone to show you where the photocopier is, where to find a pen, or even how to put in that vacation request. Throwing your weight around (even if you were hired to fulfill a managerial position) will not help you learn the job any faster. You are going to need help to survive this new workplace.

Be amiable with those around you and appreciative of their effort to help you acclimate. Pushing your way in or immediately making changes will ensure that you are not well liked right off the bat. Now, if you were hired to make changes immediately, this is a different story. But it is still in your best interest to know how things work currently before making changes to the workplace.

LEARNING THE JOB TAKES TIME

Don't be too hard on yourself. Even if you have done similar work before, learning a new job takes time. Again, it takes at least a year to learn a job, another year to get better at the job, and another year to start improving the job. By years four and five, you can cut corners and find efficiencies. By year six, you are probably doing the equivalent volume of work of two people. You aren't the new person anymore and can train new employees on your work team.

No employer in their right mind expects a new person to be functioning at the same level as an employee who has been there for ten years. Of course, you are always expected to hit milestones as you progress, such as a certain level of knowledge by three months and another level of knowledge by the end of the first year. If you can't hit these milestones, ask for help; it's better to reach out to a colleague or boss than to fall behind. Spend your time making sure you completely understand what you are expected to do. Not only does this look good to your boss, but it improves your skill set and expands your résumé.

To be honest, a new job always sucks at first. Personally, whenever I have a new job, I privately declare I'm going to quit every day for the first month.

PaRt two

THE HUNT DOESN'T STOP

Though you have a job now, the hunt doesn't stop. Hunters are always looking for the next meal, or, in this case, a job. They look after their own best interests, ensuring they remain on top of their game. The phrase "use it or lose it" is very apt here. Maybe you don't want a new job right now, and it's okay to be comfortable, but it doesn't hurt to see what else is out there.

If you're the one looking for employees, you get a very different view of the hunting process. In fact, becoming an interviewer strengthens your skills as an interviewee.

This section takes a walk through an employer's point of view. Considering this perspective can only strengthen your experience on the other side of the table.

THE OTHER SIDE OF THE TABLE

One day in the future, you may be the one on the selection side of the table; your view of the hiring process will change, dramatically, and you will realize it's not easy. Before being the interviewer, you might've thought, *What's so hard about hiring? Just get it done, hire the most qualified, and move on.* But hiring the right person takes a lot of effort. There are so many dimensions that you have never considered before. The person you eventually hire must have the technical skills to do the job, but they also need a personality that matches what you are looking and the ability to fit in with the workplace culture and the team already in place. Sometimes, you need to hire someone who could eventually do *your* job—and considering your potential replacement is not an easy thing to do.

The hunt for employees requires so many different considerations. When you hunt for yourself, you only need to consider what you want or need. When hunting for an employee, you must take into account all employees, the whole of the company.

Employers do not merely look for the most technically qualified. If that were the case, they could tap into all post-secondary institutions and hire the top five in each class—problem solved. In a perfect world, that would be the most straightforward course of action for any potential employer. But while technical skills are fundamental, the reality is that employees most likely get hired based on how well they answered the softer questions. The decision could be as simple as likeability. Your credentials, education, and experience got you to the interview level, but book smarts do not automatically equal the best employee. What gets you the job is how well you *fit.*

"Fit" refers to whether the person can intertwine technical skills and personability. As mentioned before, as a potential employer, you will see what "The decision is made in the first thirty seconds" means. You will start to get a feel for who can do the job and who will struggle from day one. The secret is to give people the benefit of the doubt. Your candidate might blow the first few minutes but turn the interview around and become the best person for the job.

Always account for nerves when interviewing a candidate. This could be another measure of skill and attitude. Can this person handle or react appropriately to intense situations? There is no reason why you can't help them along a bit. Perhaps they are going through a personal issue, and their nerves reflect that. Change the question, rephrase it, or break it into smaller pieces. Ask another question and give them time to respond accordingly. People might find their groove halfway through the interview.

If the person still doesn't get it, they may not be the right person. Use your judgment—is it *every* question, or do they need a minute to acclimate to the interview setting? There are many questions to ask, many opportunities for them to excel. They could do well answering nine out of ten questions, so don't judge on one unsatisfactory answer. After all, you should know what that feels like. You've been on the other side.

HIRING THE RIGHT PEOPLE

Staffing your team or workplace with the right people is a job in and of itself. You need to determine the specific tasks you want people to do and the outcomes you expect to achieve. What do you need, what can you do with the team you have, and why do you need more people? You may be in a panic, and there may be deliverables you need to meet, but what if you only need short-term help? You also need to ask yourself how long it will be until they are effective and producing at the level you need them to.

Hiring mistakes happen when you are unsure of what you need or are in a rush to hire. You may not take the time to ensure you have hired someone who fits the job and the workplace. After all, remember, some people take a job just because they need one. These employees may or may not be invested in doing a good job. Sometimes a bad hire is not just one person's mistake. Maybe the applicant misunderstood the job requirements, the employer didn't fully explain what they were looking for in an employee, the job itself changed direction, or maybe when the original hire happened, the employer had no idea what they needed.

Don't rush and hire the wrong person. Keep in mind that there are always people who don't come to work for the same reasons you do. Sometimes, a person's problems follow them into the workplace. You need to use your backbone and let go of these types (or not hire them in the first place). You and your business do not need the aggravation.

WHAT SHOULD YOU BE LOOKING FOR?

Before you start your first advertisement, there are several questions you need to ask yourself:

- Do you want someone who can simply produce extra work?
- Are you concerned with how they fit into your existing organization?
- Do you need someone temporarily or someone who will stay long-term?
- Are you looking for someone who wants the simple nine-to-five gig or a person who wants to grow?
- Do you want someone with the same values as your company?
- What's more important to you: experience or education?

Each of these items is something you need to explore as you consider hiring someone. You may ask yourself many more questions. To get the right person in place, you need to fully outline what you expect from this person and what you need them to do. It doesn't do anyone any good to simply hire a person to do *something* when you can't define the duties. The person you hire will most likely get frustrated and move on, and you will be in the same boat—looking to hire, still unaware of what you need. It can be a vicious cycle.

TAKE YOUR TIME

Maybe you need to hire someone because of an overflow of work. Maybe a position has been vacant for some time and you have taken on that vacancy's responsibilities. Or there is a new line of business in your company and you need people to grow that department. Merely hiring bodies will eventually come back to bite you. This may be sufficient for short-term employees or a limited-time project, but you don't want someone just keeping a chair warm when searching for long-term staff.

You need a person who is going to be interested in working and doing a good job. You don't want someone who will suck up resources and be a drain on the company. You may be better off with no one rather than a bad hire who will cause problems in the long run. It would be prudent to search for a solution other than hiring if you know you're going to be rushed. There are always other short-term solutions that don't create long-term issues.

Take the time to review a person through many different lenses, not just their technical skills. This also means reviewing more than a person's résumé. Look at how they present themselves and how they respond to questions. Although you do need to be concerned with the cost of hiring and the impact of not having enough employees to deliver, you should also be selective about who is representing your company. There isn't always the luxury of time; however, a few checks and balances will save you future pain.

TECHNICALLY SOUND

Looking for an employee who is technically sound should be a given. Many jobs have technical requirements, such as a position as an engineer or an accountant. As you look for an employee, make sure they have the skills they say they do, and be specific as to what skills you need. If you need someone who can do payroll, then state that. If you need someone who can read detailed drawings or schematics, articulate that. Use industry-specific jargon to describe your needs. When you are looking for a generalist, be clear and specific; the language and job duties should be clearly understood.

> **YOU NEED PEOPLE WHO CAN ACTUALLY DO THE JOB YOU NEED THEM TO DO.**

Candidates need to be able to demonstrate their skills—with samples of their work, a presentation on a subject, or by providing examples of how they have used their knowledge. If you know someone who used to work with this person, ask whether their work represents a standard you would find acceptable.

It is only to your benefit to confirm someone can do the job they say they can. If you need to test them several times to be sure, do so. The last thing you need is someone who has no idea what they are doing.

APPLICANT'S UNDERSTANDING

It doesn't hurt to ask a candidate their understanding of the position requirements. This allows you, as the hiring manager, an opportunity to gauge the applicant's knowledge of the written job description and their understanding of the job they applied for. This conversation will also tell you how much research the applicant did ahead of time. You will be able to determine how invested the applicant is in their career. If the applicant simply repeats the job posting or tells you what you want to hear, this means they can memorize words from an advertisement, not that they can necessarily conceptualize or apply knowledge.

If they can articulate in their own words an understanding of the job that is close to your ideas, you might have a good candidate. And if you describe the job and they can't repeat it back to you in their own words, then cut your losses—this is not the candidate for you. There are too many occasions when people quit a job because it wasn't what they thought it was. If you want to hire someone to support strategic communications, make sure they have a communications background. You shouldn't necessarily accept someone who applied just because they like working with people; that tells you they probably have no idea what the job entails.

Determining whether the applicant understands the job benefits both interviewer and interviewee. Spend more time in the interview if you need to. If you're not on the same page, then there isn't much point moving forward with the conversation. Set clear expectations during the interview to avoid problems moving forward.

AVOID BUZZ SKILLS

Employers may become entranced by a well-written résumé or by someone who can knock an interview out of the park. An applicant could be a whiz at using all the proper terminology and telling the potential employer just what they want to hear, but there might be little substance behind those words. Sometimes what seems like the best candidate is your worst. All splash, no waves. All fluff, no cake. All bun, no hot dog. These candidates will use words as a strategy to seem appealing for the position. They will speak about teamwork as though they understand it, whereas, in reality, they could be more like a lone wolf. They talk about perspective as though they practice looking at things from another side; in actuality, they rarely consider other's actions.

As an employer, you need to dig into their answers. Ask additional questions, make them talk more about their understanding of the company and their role, and probe a bit to see if you can poke holes in their responses. If they truly know what they are talking about and can support their answer with examples, then you might have a winner. If your candidate starts to become uncomfortable, stutters, or can't provide an example, then you have just called *bullshit* on them. If your candidate can't support their responses, there is likely no substance to their answers, and they don't understand the job.

As an employer, watch out for overused words applicants sometimes use. Here's what they really mean:

- Leadership—this does not mean what people think it does. Lead what and lead whom? What did you lead, and how? Leadership should be about motivating people. Telling people what to do is not leading.

- Strategic—this is the most overused word in the last two decades; it has lost all its meaning.
- Excellent—how do you know the work is excellent? By whose measure?
- Passionate—people can be passionate about some things, maybe a cause or portions of their work, but it's rare for someone to be passionate about working a nine-to-five job.
- Creative—by whose standards? One person's creativity is another's day-to-day work.
- Specialized—specialized in what way, and by whose standards? If they don't include examples, it's really just a fanciful word.
- Focused—this should be a requirement of all employees (therefore, it isn't necessary to list as a skill).

Don't get sucked in by the flashy word or skill of the day. If someone says they are an expert at something, ask them to provide examples of how they've used this skill in the past. Within their response, see if they can prove it to you. Otherwise, you are just getting an expert at spinning tales.

REAL SKILLS YOU SHOULD BE LOOKING FOR

Many employers spend a lot of time and effort looking for a laundry list of technical skills. While technical skills are essential (because they need to know what they are doing and speak your industry's language), this is only half the story. You want someone with the ability to learn—who's willing and able to grow as the company does. You need someone who can change direction if something isn't working right. You need someone who can recognize when an error has been made and take steps to correct it. You need someone capable of making improvements and asking hard questions. Mostly, you need someone who isn't afraid to make changes, even if there is the possibility of losing their job.

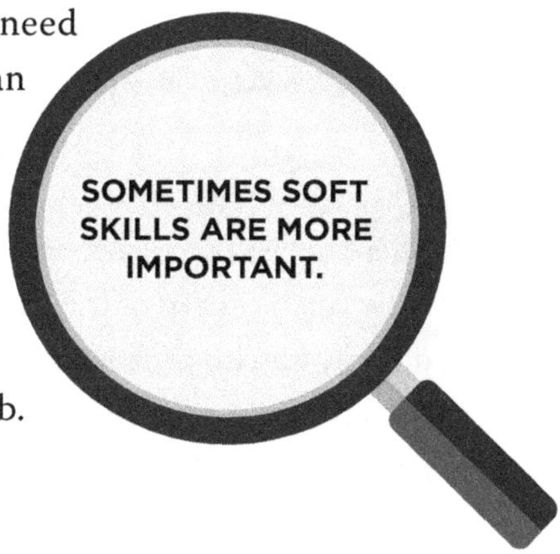

CULTURE

As you look to hire a new person, consider that you already have a cohesive group of people. This group of people works well together, understands each other's quirks, has a good rapport with each other, and is already working as a team. Bringing in a new person while also saying goodbye to an old person will disrupt that dynamic even more. The team will feel the loss of a team member and may resent someone else taking their place. The person being replaced could have left for various reasons. However, they had their place set within the team.

The new team member may be measured against the person who left. They will struggle to fill the long-term employee's shoes; but this is not what they should be doing. As an employer, you need to find a balance between bringing in new ideas and finding someone who fits with the existing team. If you find someone who is the same, no new perspectives will be introduced. You want someone who can stand on their own and be brave enough to go against the group when they need to but also be able to work with the team when the situation calls for it.

In most situations, workplace norms are established. Ensure your new hire can work within these norms. Provide some orientation of the culture of the workplace. You could assign another employee to show your new staff member the ropes. Essentially, you need to hire someone who the team is willing to accept and who may offer positive new team dynamics.

PERSONALITY FIT

You're going to come to a point when it comes down to personality. There may be several candidates who meet the technical requirements. Now you have two or three people who will do the job as advertised. But do they fit with the rest of your team? Perhaps one of these candidates is technically sound but arrogant and self-absorbed. You will have to ask yourself what is most important to you. Do you want a team that can work together and not create workplace drama? Maybe you have a great workplace where everyone pulls together and works as a team, but it takes very little to upset the balance. One poisonous pill can ruin the work environment in a brief period.

Your decision may simply depend on likeability. Once all other criteria are out of the way, this is your best method to pick someone who will fit or complement your team. Maybe you ask your team who they like the best and let them choose. Remember, this is the team you depend on to meet your business outcomes or objectives. Do you want to spend time dealing with personality conflicts and drama rather than getting real work done?

WORK ETHIC

Work ethic is hard to discern from an interview. You could phrase your questions to gain some idea of their ethics. It's probably not a good idea to ask, "Hey, do you steal?" but you could pose a scenario where a person would have to make an ethical choice. They will most likely use past experiences to support their responses. Through the experiences they share, you can gauge their ethical position and what kind of person you're hiring. Did they follow the procedure or do their own thing? Did they perform their job safely? Did they follow directions from their boss?

Historically, exhibiting unethical behaviour has sometimes been viewed as simply a part of doing business. However, today, it is less tolerated and much easier to uncover. Every action is documented via some form of technology. There is always a record. Someone, somewhere, someday will find out all your dirty secrets. Honesty is always the best policy; if you suspect the candidate is dishonest, don't hire them.

A LOYAL EMPLOYEE

Loyalty is a commodity. It's necessary to establish when first hiring an employee, and most definitely when retaining an employee. People who hop from one job to the next are not loyal employees. You need people who stick out the job and improve it. Loyalty means people care about the business, their job, and the customers or clients they serve.

People look for a new job for all sorts of reasons. You can tell by their résumé if they have any level of loyalty. Look at how long they spent at their previous jobs; if every job is less than two years (and they weren't contract jobs or high school or college summer jobs), then you probably have a job-hopper. Where possible, look for someone who has stayed at least five or six years at one company (assuming this isn't an entry-level position and you're not dealing with new graduates). Just to drive this point home, it takes at least one year to learn a job, at least a year to get better at the job, and another year to make the job more efficient. In total, that's a minimum of three years at a job; after three years, you can generally assume the employee is established, efficient, and loyal.

SELF-STARTER

Sometimes there's a problem in the workplace but you're not sure how to fix it as an employer. You need employees who are willing to bring issues to your attention, but you also need them to offer solutions, options, alternatives, and perspectives. You want someone who thinks of ways to improve or expand the business. These employees will be able to bring forward new ideas while also being able to provide a risk-benefit analysis of their ideas—outlining the pros, the cons, and the ways to achieve success. They should also be able to identify impacts on current business. This doesn't mean you have to accept every idea put forward. But it does mean you have an employee who can think. It also means you have a repository of ideas you can draw on in the future if necessary.

Having a self-starter also means that you don't have to watch over your employees on a day-to-day basis. They should be able to work with minimal supervision. The person you hire should be able to conduct themselves professionally, identify their daily work and the information they need to achieve desired outcomes, and meet deadlines—all with very little interference on your part.

WHAT DON'T YOU WANT?

You spend a lot of time trying to figure out what kind of employee you want. Now consider what kind of a person you don't want. Think about the worst coworker you have ever worked with; think about their knowledge, their ability to get along with others, or their work ethic. Once you have that image in your head, hire the exact opposite. You don't want someone who causes dissension, doesn't do their work, or annoys the rest of the staff. You don't want to be in a position where your company values and ethics are called into question because of one employee's actions. Spend just as much time figuring out what you *don't* want as you do figuring out what you *do* want. If you need to, make a list of the traits you want in an employee and a list of the characteristics you don't want. It's a simple exercise and very low-tech, but it might help focus your thoughts. Any little bit of assistance will prove beneficial in this lengthy process.

THE HUNTING GROUNDS

You are now at the point where you have decided on the skills you need in a candidate; you have an outline of the work you need them to do, you know the education you need them to have, you know the traits you are looking for, and you know what you don't want. Now you need to find this perfect person who will fill these requirements. You know how they will hunt for a job because that's how you got your job.

You need to decide on your budget. How much do you want to spend on advertising? Are you looking for free sites or within a specific industry? There are options to advertise within particular associations. Industry-specific associations usually offer space to advertise upcoming jobs to their members. If you want a new graduate, you could consider promoting your job opportunity at universities or colleges. There are always student unions willing to assist fellow students in landing that dream job.

There are also traditional methods. How about a newspaper ad? Those do still exist. Newspapers are also electronic, so you could pay for an ad there as well. There is also an extremely low-tech option, like putting up a sign in the window of your business. This option produces results; people who shop at your business could be looking for a job or have friends who are looking for a job. Word of mouth is the best social media out there. Your current employees are likewise a solid form of advertising. They have a network of people within the same industry who may be interested in the job, and it's a big compliment if your staff are happy enough to suggest friends for the position.

Social media sites, if well managed, are also a source to find applicants. You can create short, snappy ads that will draw the attention of job hunters. Whoever sees the ad may not be in the market for a new job, but they might know someone who is and can easily share the details.

If you have a large budget, you can pay an agency to hire on your behalf. You can lay out all your needs, and they do the advertising and screen the employees for you. They could take the stress out of the process and simply send you a few top candidates to interview. Similarly, headhunting agencies can scout out contenders for the position, though these should be reserved for hard-to-fill or executive-level positions (but they're always an option).

MONITORING THE HUNT

Personally, I'm not a big proponent of social networking sites. Given the nature of these sites, it's hard to discern truth from fiction. Some people have different personas online; what is projected through posts is not necessarily who they are. Others are true to form; if they are an ass in person, they might be an ass online.

Some employers check up on a potential employee's social media profiles, eager to see their online personality. While it's not a bad thing to do, I wouldn't recommend it as an immediate first step to their hire. You might be able to garner some useful information from those sites as a last resort—maybe confirmation of past work experience or other experiences the candidate has said they have. But if you depend on a social media profile to determine a candidate's fit, you do both yourself and the candidate a disservice.

There is also the option of simply plugging your candidate's name into a search engine. You never know what you're going to find.

Most people don't put every single professional aspect of their lives on a specific site. Searching could yield things like papers they've written, collaborations they have undertaken, or causes they have volunteered for. You could learn a whole lot through a simple search. You might also find things you never needed to know.

People have a right to their personal life, even if it doesn't jibe with yours. You should be concerned with how they professionally conduct themselves during your working hours. Can they competently complete the tasks assigned to them? Do they demonstrate loyalty to their place of employment? What people do in their social time is their business. Their actions are not a reflection of the company or its values unless they contradict the employment guidelines. Though scrutiny of social media is absolutely something to expect on your own job hunt, you really shouldn't be using personal opinions, associations, or views as a method to screen people out.

HUNTING EXPENSES

Filling a vacancy is an expensive undertaking, meaning it requires a lot of effort. First, you have a vacancy because someone has left the company, which means there is a reduction in productivity. The search for the right candidate is much like searching for a job. It would help if you did your research. Are you going to leave it to fate, hoping the right candidate will show up on your doorstep? It could happen, but most likely, it won't. You will need to advertise—on traditional newspapers (costly), on social media (not monetarily expensive but costly in time spent), and on your company website (this is the right choice, but very static, unless there are candidates who want to work for you specifically). Job boards are good but could get lost in the thousands of jobs listed. Headhunters are very expensive and should only be used for executive positions.

Once you've advertised and have a good selection of candidates, where else does it get expensive? Your own time is again a cost. It takes time to review résumés. If you have a large number of applications, that's a lot of reading on your part. Once you have narrowed down the original submissions, you need to interview—more time and money. Interview appointments can take up half a day; then you realize that you'll have to conduct another round of interviews the next day. That's a lot of time and productivity lost.

Once you make a decision and hire someone—great!—you have to train them and get them to a level where they can be a fully productive team member. From the time you identify a need for a position to the point where the employee is a fully functioning member of your team is, give or take, one full year. To repeat: *hiring requires a lot of time and money.* While it takes more time in the moment to make sure you're hiring the right person, it saves you the hassle of going through this process several times. Choose wisely.

AGE VERSUS EXPERIENCE

When looking for someone to fill a position, you may run into a common dilemma: age versus experience. Do you hire someone fresh out of school with minimal work experience? Or do you hire a person with many years of experience who might retire within a short period? There is no right or wrong answer to this. Both are good decisions. It comes down to what you need. Do you need new blood and new ideas? Or do you need someone who can step in with little mentoring required, who can get started quickly, understand the job, and make changes with little support? If you have the time to mentor, then maybe the right decision is to hire a relatively inexperienced person to mould into a long-haul employee.

When a job advertisement states that the company is looking for someone with relevant experience, they probably don't want to have to train anyone. Some closely related industries can easily cross over to another aspect of a business. Transferable skills are knowledge that a person takes with them wherever they go; these skills are not necessarily learned and are valuable to have in an employee.

People who learn as they go can still be valuable to a business. Not every employer sees their value, but teachability is certainly an important aspect to consider before hiring someone. Keep in mind that transferable skills can come from either past work experience or education.

BENEFITS OF HIRING EXPERIENCE

Hiring a more seasoned employee brings all sorts of benefits. They have years of experience and knowledge. They can generally be at full capacity in a short period. They don't need a lot of hand-holding and can usually figure out the job's needs reasonably quickly. Seasoned employees are in a great position to be an informal mentor to a younger or less experienced employee. These employees are probably more available than the area manager and can help with everyday issues and concerns. There is also usually less drama with a seasoned employee. They just want to work and contribute without getting involved in the politics of the workplace.

However, hiring experience can come with its challenges. You may have an older employee who is stuck in their ways and not interested in trying anything new. This perspective could lead to challenges within the workplace if left unmanaged.

Your seasoned employee may not intend to stay long on the job. This job may be their second career, or they just want a job until they are fully ready to retire. These are not bad circumstances, only something to consider. As long as you have a dependable employee who is not interested in leading the younger generation astray, you can take advantage of their experience in the time they are with you.

THE LESS EXPERIENCED EMPLOYEE

There is something to be said for new, inexperienced employees. They introduce fresh ideas and values into a potentially stagnant workgroup, not only in terms of the actual work but also to the workplace culture. Freshly out of school with minimal work experience, this person could also provide updates to employees who may not have been in school for quite some time.

However, hiring a less experienced employee brings its own set of challenges. More effort on the part of the manager is usually required to support the new employee. They may need more supervision or guidance, simply because they don't have the work history to draw upon for reference. They may also have higher expectations based on their generation. Some may expect a higher percentage of the boss's time; some may have expectations of advancement within a short period. Managing the expectations of a new, younger, or less experienced employee will take time and effort; as an employer, you need to decide where your efforts will provide the most benefit. This is not to say that less experienced employees can't get there. As an employer, it's incumbent on you to set up your new employees for success.

WHAT YOU SHOULD BE ASKING

You want someone who can do the tasks you require. If they made it through the interview, they most likely have all the necessary educational and technical requirements to do the job. Through your screening process, you want to learn what kind of person you are hiring. Remember that you will spend eight to ten hours a day with this person. You rely on employees to meet the needs of your customers. It's easy to simply ask questions of a potential candidate, but to gain a true understanding of work habits, you may need to think outside the box. Because we are all human beings, we all have our own perspectives based on our lived experience. These experiences influence how we interpret the expectations of a job. Thus, it is prudent, as an employer, to really consider what you should be asking of a future employee who will support your business.

REFERENCE CHECK—YAY OR NAY?

Is there value in a reference check? Sometimes. After all, most potential employees will not provide the name of someone who would give a bad reference. Then you have to wonder if the person you're talking to just wants to get rid of this employee. Or you might get lucky and receive an accurate and honest review of your candidate's work.

Sometimes the references are not up to date. Maybe your candidate worked for this person ten years ago. That's not an accurate representation of how this candidate performs today. Your best bet for a good reference is to phone past supervisors. Alternatively, an informal check on a person sometimes yields helpful information. You could ask if anyone knows the work habits of your potential candidate, thereby validating your formal reference checks.

WHAT DO YOU EXPECT OF YOUR BOSS?

Employees and employers need to be on the same page. Work styles differ between individuals, and you may need to adjust to meet those needs. You may be the type of boss who gives high-level instruction and expects the staff to figure out how to get there. But your team may need explicit detail in every step. If neither of you states your needs, you will run into miscommunication.

The simple way to solve this is to ask, "As my employee, what are your expectations of me as your boss?" It might be a bit uncomfortable to have this kind of conversation, but it can save you some grief in the long run. This kind of discussion sets the ground rules and expectations for communication right from the start. You each know your role and what to do. You each can speak up if something isn't going right. And you get your working relationship off to a good start. This conversation will help in developing rapport right out of the gate. You understand each other's needs to be successful and tailor your approach accordingly.

WHAT ARE YOUR EXPECTATIONS FOR THE JOB?

As previously stated, there are times when the employer and the employee have very different job expectations. If you thought you hired someone to build widgets, but they are building gadgets instead, then wires were crossed somewhere. As you go through the process of hiring someone, make sure your expectations are clear. Their responsibilities should be clear. It doesn't hurt, during the interview, to outline your expectations of the job. Sometimes, you might need to give your prospective employee the complete lowdown of what they are getting themselves into.

Be very explicit in your description of the job duties and the challenges this position might face. The idea is to eliminate any surprises for your potential candidate without scaring them off. Share the working styles of those in your work unit. Share the projects this position would be expected to complete. While you may already have an extraordinarily driven and high-functioning team of employees, this new person needs to know as much information as possible beforehand so they can fit in seamlessly.

REFLECTIONS

The hunt for employment and the hunt for an employee is almost the same, requiring a lot of work and effort to find the perfect fit. Success is contingent upon building a relationship with someone you just met.

Here are a few reminders:

- Get good at writing your résumé; the volume of jobs you apply for will surprise you. Writing a résumé is not a one-and-done kind of thing. The job hunt could last a lifetime (unless you find your dream job early in your career).
- Keep your résumé updated. It's much easier to keep adding to your résumé as you obtain new work than it is to try to remember each job you've had. It doesn't mean you need it or are actively searching for work. Adding information when it's fresh is just good practice. Always having a current résumé means all you have to do is write a new cover letter. It's a time-saver.
- Staying in a job is not a bad thing. Just because you find something you like does not mean you are stagnant; don't let anyone tell you differently. If you are happy where you are and are doing the work you love, then there is no reason to move.

- There will be lots of rejection. You may put out 100 résumés and only receive one job offer. You will most likely feel terrible each time you receive a rejection letter. Perseverance is the best way to succeed.
- Neither interviewing nor being interviewed are fun activities. Both involve some nerves; the interviewee is trying to make a good impression, and the interviewer is hoping this last interview will be the one that works out.
- Don't give up. A good fit is out there, possibly your dream job. Don't let one rejection discourage you from applying to other opportunities.
- Broaden your search. Be inventive in the search for an employee or for employment. Sticking with what you know is the safe road, and that's okay. But a little out-of-the-box thinking could be to your benefit.
- Job hunting is a lot harder than it used to be. It's about showcasing your skills and talents, which doesn't always mean your education. What do you have that no one else does?

At a minimum, my hope for *The Hunt* is that you come away knowing you are not alone in your struggles to find employment or an employee. There are tools and resources available to help you in your hunt; you may just need to be inventive to find them. *The Hunt* doesn't cover every possible scenario to help you, but it does crack that door open.

ACKNOWLEDGMENTS

To my children, Matthew and Kayla, thank you for not listening to me. Neither of you thought I knew what I was talking about in your hunt for a job. Your endless questions about what everything means and what you need to do throughout the process inspired me to write about everything we talked about and then some. Dave, as always, your support means everything.

Theresa, thank you again for your red pen, advice, and input into what should be included in *The Hunt*. Without you, I probably wouldn't have completed this book. Jennifer C, your perspective and encouragement were so helpful as I struggled with writer's block. Wendy, as always, your friendship over these many, many years gets me through every hurdle. And Koehler Books, thank you for taking a chance on me.

OTHER BOOKS BY JENNIFER FLORAX

The book every novice employee needs to read, *Survival Guide for the Working World: What School Doesn't Teach You*, offers tips, tricks, and bite-sized bits to equip those entering and navigating the workforce. Combining a bit of humour with some serious conversation, the ultimate goal of this book is to make the transition from student to employee less of a shock to the system.

CPSIA information can be obtained
at www.ICGtesting.com
Printed in the USA
LVHW100113250922
729205LV00022B/492

9 781646 636914